The Startup Marketing Bible

A PRACTICAL GUIDE
TO STARTUP MARKETING

Kenny Sahr

Published 2019 by Kenny Sahr

Herzliya, Israel

kenny@sahr.com

To my family, for their love and support

Contents

Introduction   1

Marketing's Role During Every Startup Stage   3

How Marketing Works With Other C-Levels   13

A Journey Through the Marketing-Sales Funnel   20

Decision Makers and Influencers   27

A Startup's First Website   34

The Marketing Budget   42

Essential Marketing Tools   47

Meet the Marketing Vendors   64

Content   71

Social Media   90

Public Relations   95

Campaigns   99

Conferences   109

How to Track and Analyze Results   115

Marketing Best Practices Per Sector   122

Agile Startup Marketing   136

8 Signs Your Startup is in Trouble!   141

A Passion For Technology   146

Risk and Reward   154

About the Author   157

Introduction

I founded my first internet business in 1995 – web design, hosting and internet services. We had a T1 line which was a challenge for the phone company to install in Coral Gables, Florida. Every business needed a website – essentially an online business card with a contact page. We did the coding, content and graphics manually and with software that ran on Windows 95.

I realized the importance of content early on and founded my own content website in 1996. I used Notepad to create pages. Within months, I learned how to sell ads and made sure my users submitted new content and that every page was filled with profitable ads.

Google Analytics didn't exist in 1996. Sometimes advertisers had their own ad tracking and sometimes we agreed on a third party tool. Banner servers were primitive in the 1990's. Changing an ad banner meant downloading the entire site, running a mass search and replace, and uploading the site again.

I learned to improve the ad banners that my advertisers gave me. If I could improve the clickthrough rate from 2% to 5%, they would consider increasing spending and agree on a long-term deal.

The business lasted 18 years - much longer than I expected. For two decades, I was discovering and innovating on my own and didn't know the proper names of the things I was doing – landing pages, conversions, marketing automation.

When I look back, while today's marketing landscape is more complex, it is also easier – there are solutions for nearly every challenge. Marketing a startup before WordPress and Google Analytics existed required a lot of technical knowledge.

The foundations of startup marketing – website, content and campaigns – have each spawned new professions and specialties. One thing hasn't changed – startups are small and marketing professionals have a lot to deal with.

In this book, my goal is to provide you with a broad, concise and practical guide to startup marketing. Every chapter here can justify a book. While writing this book, I thought of the startup professional who doesn't have time to read a long series of books.

I hope this book helps you to hit the ground running!

CHAPTER 1

Marketing's Role During Every Startup Stage

A startup goes through a few stages in its lifecycle. It begins with an idea by the founders. Before any paperwork is filed, the founders build a prototype of their idea and gain valuable insight from friends and colleagues. If the idea holds promise and they know the right people, angel investors will fund the startup with "seed money". Seed money is often called the "friends and family stage". Usually the sum invested at this early stage is in the hundreds of thousands of dollars to a few million dollars.

Startups at the seed stage can also be considered in "stealth mode". Sounds like James Bond. Stealth mode startups are working on a secret product and don't want anyone to know the details. Some stealth mode startups have single page websites that tease their big idea. Many people on LinkedIn have "stealth mode startup" on their profile.

The Clock is Ticking

Once the first investment goes through, the clock is ticking. Many people don't realize this, but the startup is in debt. A few times a year, a typical startup will require more seed money to continue. The startup

CEO has two roles – to continue developing the idea into a solid product and to make sure the startup is funded.

With seed money, the startup's R&D & product teams grow. The first employees will usually run the teams and become senior management. "Senior management" at a startup is a confusing title. In reality, the directors and vice presidents at startups spend 95% of their time rolling up their sleeves and doing grunt work. They spend the remaining 5% of their time as executives, going to meetings and managing processes. The first ones in are building the startup's infrastructure and foundation.

The Elevator Pitch

Marketing's role at the early stage is to build the marketing foundation. Start with your elevator pitch. How do you communicate your startup in 30 seconds or less to technology and business professionals? Create a document with your elevator pitch and get input from your team members. Develop different versions of your elevator pitch for different audiences – technology, business, investors and one for "everyone else". Test your "everyone else" elevator pitch to friends and family who don't work in technology. Test the other versions on those you and your team meet in the initial months and fine tune it.

The Product & Technology

Now that you have conjured up an elevator pitch, it is time to develop the pitch into content. Create a document that describes and illustrates your product. Create another document for your technology. Discuss it with your startup team members. Edit these documents until you and whoever else you are working with are satisfied with the results. These two documents will be the basis of your website content, printed brochures and even press releases.

Once you have quality product and technology documents, you can fill in the blanks and create more content. Whatever you need – a press release, datasheet, an email to a potential customer or investor – you have a source for the core content.

Create a master PowerPoint for investors. Your CEO will ask for this. Half of it will be product and technology, and the other half will cover the opportunity at hand. Every piece of content that you produce adds to your collection of assets.

The Website

Once you have written and assembled your first content assets, you are ready to create your startup's website. I cover this in detail in another chapter. In this section, I want to stress that the website is usually created at the seed stage, and sometimes immediately after Series A investment.

The first iteration of a startup's website can be basic – 10-15 pages of content that targets future investors and decision makers. The goal isn't to create the most comprehensive website, but to build the foundation so you can add content (pages) later.

The Funnel

With the website comes the funnel. If you have a sales team or person, the website project is the green light for developing your startup's marketing-sales funnel. The stakeholders are the CEO, VP Sales and VP Marketing plus of course the founders. A startup has to have a clear marketing-sales funnel and a website that provides relevant content and captures leads.

A Few Notes on the Seed Stage

Working at a startup at the seed stage is like entering the twilight zone. Unlike almost every business around you, you have zero sales, zero income and a lot of promise. There is a tendency for people to "live large" and go shopping for non-essential things on other people's money. Be careful. Your startup is on life support and is burning through a lot of cash. The "burn rate" – how much your startup is spending per month/quarter – determines how much time you have until you run out of money.

Another common issue that comes up at seed stage startups has to do with remote working. Every new company creates a work culture in its first months and first year. Decide what kind of culture you want at your startup and work with others to make it happen. Remote work is fine, but there are limits to everything. There is no replacement for real-life meetings.

Startup Twilight Zone

I was at an early stage startup that was happily spending friends and family investments for over 4 years. That's a lot of time to spend in the twilight zone! We were allowed to work at home, but the VP Sales and I came to the office a few days a week and enjoyed the interactions. Meeting in person helped us to build a solid funnel. The VP R&D, on the other hand, only showed up for weekly meetings. Because he was never there, we rarely interacted with him.

Everyone has a different view on this. I'm somewhere in the middle – if I have the choice, I prefer to work both remotely and at the office. I know I get things done quicker at home, but I enjoy – and need – the interactions with others for practical reasons. There's a magic in real world conversations that the phone, texting and video conferencing can't replace.

Bad Behavior

The seed stage can reinforce bad behavior. Going years without customers, sales targets and income drips down to the product and R&D teams and affects everyone. In a normal company, it begins with pressure on sales to bring in income, moves down to marketing to assist sales, on down to product to create a killer product and finally onto R&D to develop a technology. The CEO sets priorities and goals for each team. The pressure to deliver results is oxygen in the business world.

When a startup has real customers, there are real people who can ask tough questions to the R&D and product teams. It opens them up to "the world". Without real customers, critiques come from a much smaller pool of people – team members, potential investors and anyone who is given a demo.

Sometimes you will see a "messiah complex" with the founders and the first employees. It's great to believe in what you are doing, but keep in mind that at this stage, you haven't earned a dollar and you are 100% untested. At one startup that I was at, you couldn't talk to any of the principals. Everyone was so sure they were sitting on a winner that they forgot to focus on customers and make sure the first customers were onboarded successfully.

Onboarding First Customers Is Critical

This leads me to my next point – onboarding the first customers is a big deal. When you get your first purchase orders, the real test of your startup begins. All hands on deck. From the CEO on down, everyone has a stake in successfully onboarding the first customers.

If your technology involves hardware and not SaaS, a few people should get on an airplane and fly to your first customers. Help them install it and learn from their first uses of your product. Even if your product is SaaS, ecommerce or something else, consider having a team on the ground to watch and learn from your first customers. Better to charge them less and learn from them than to end up earning nothing because they never use your product.

I was at a startup where I saw what happens when onboarding the first customers fails. The COO tried to do it remotely. The hardware and software were way too complex for a customer to handle on their own. Emails went back and forth. The companies eventually stopped trying to use the product.

Series A Investment

The Series A investment is a trophy for the CEO and founders. Series A means a venture capital firm or a group of seasoned investors is putting millions to tens of millions of dollars into your startup. This is when things start to get interesting!

In order to receive a Series A investment, the startup CEO presents a growth plan to the investors. They will modify it based on their experience. Once the money is in the account, the CEO gets to work on a plan to scale everything up.

Scale it Up

At the seed stage, a startup will have a small R&D team, a VP Product (or none) and a few marketing and sales professionals (at the most). After Series A, everything changes. One small R&D team grows to a few R&D teams. A product team is formed, with a defined structure connecting them to R&D. Marketing and sales teams are hired and put to work. Some startups hire their own human resources professional/s and others bring in human resources companies that specialize in startup talent acquisition. The founders themselves will settle into clearly defined roles.

If you were working remotely at the seed stage, expect to be in the office a lot more often for Series A. With dozens of employees, a startup solidifies its work culture. Now there are two external pressure points – investors and customers.

Marketing During Series A

Marketing's role during Series A is to quickly finish building the marketing infrastructure and begin scaling up. Your website and funnel should be a greased and oiled lead generation machine. If not, get it done quickly. It won't be long before your CEO and VP Sales are asking about leads.

Scaling Up Marketing

Scaling up marketing at a startup is an art and a science. By now, you know what works as far as messaging and campaign channels. Focus on your best performing campaigns and gradually raise the budget. Track results by the hour to ensure that your sweet spot remains sweet as campaign money flows out.

Communicate constantly with your sales team and make sure they are receiving quality inbound leads from marketing. Are the new scaled up campaigns converting to sales as well as they should? If not, where are things slowing down?

At the same time you are scaling up campaigns, you will need to scale up your content creation efforts. If during the seed stage, one or two of you were able to improvise and write the content, Series A requires a content writer – or a few. You are also likely to need one or more campaign managers and even a social media professional on your marketing team.

You want to spend a lot of cash on campaigns, but in order to run effective campaigns, you need an ongoing cycle of new content to feed the campaigns.

Another chunk of your budget will be going to your CRM and other marketing tools. At Series A, you are scaling them up as well. Perhaps moving from a basic CRM to Salesforce, upgrading Salesforce, adding Marketo or Hubspot to the picture. Whatever you were spending and doing at seed stage you will be spending and doing more from Series A and onward.

Notes on Series A

Every election, politicians tell us that "this election is the most important ever". Likewise, every stage that a startup experiences is the most important ever. Series A is no different. By now your startup has proven that not only does it have a technology, it has a solid product that people and/or companies will buy.

Starting with Series A, the goal is to scale up revenues while scaling up product features. A small startup is morphing into a not-so-small startup. There are human resources professionals, new rules, new people and a totally different vibe than when the startup was having meetings at a local diner.

In the movies, a super hero comes in and saves the day. At startups, the CEO is the super hero. The right CEO at a newly minted Series A startup will make or break it. The experience that the startup CEO gained during the seed stage is critical. I've worked with excellent CEO's who knew how to inspire the team and get everyone onboard with the game plan.

Series B and Beyond

Most startups go through a few series of institutional investments. By Series B, the startup is raking in serious cash and has even more ambitious growth plans. The startup's teams are scaled up and are running on automatic. The startup is hopefully settling into a routine of success and constant growth.

Series B investors (and onward) are often strategic investors. They bring in money and something else. That something else can be a strategic partner to work with or merge into, or it can be an exit strategy, which leads us to the next section.

The Startup Exit

One day, you wake up to gossip on the WhatsApp Group. Did someone say exit?! The exit is the final goal and achievement of a startup. An exit is literally an IPO, buyout or merger. Whatever it is, it is big – often hundreds of millions to billions of dollars.

The founders, investors and first employees usually have stock in the startup and they are compensated for the risk they took. Hopefully the other employees get something for their risk and efforts. The formula is simple – the longer you are at a startup, the more stock you will own. Shares are distributed to employees over time to encourage everyone to stay onboard.

If you are lucky, you will experience one or more exits during your career. The exit is a crowning achievement for everyone involved.

CHAPTER 2

How Marketing Works With Other C-Levels

Every startup has its own version of senior management. Startup C-Levels are expected to excel at whatever it is they do, hands-on. Once investments and success kick in, a startup's C-Levels begin to work like C-Levels by managing people and processes.

In this section, I will discuss who is who and how marketing professionals interact with them at a startup.

CEO

The startup CEO has two main roles. First and foremost is getting investments and keeping the startup afloat. At the seed stage, this is like serving in the House of Representatives, where members face re-election every two years – the CEO is in a never-ending "funding cycle". It doesn't take long for a startup to burn through a few hundred thousand dollars of seed money. A new investment buys quiet for a few quarters at a time.

The second role of the startup CEO is to shepherd the startup from one stage to the next. At the seed stage, while working on getting seed funding, the CEO is positioning the startup for a large Series A venture capital investment. Preparing a seed stage startup for VC money means developing a technology into a product. Venture Capital investors know exactly what they are looking for.

A meandering startup without a set-in-stone market and product map won't get Series A funding. A good CEO will bring in someone with a strong product background in order to transform R&D's wonderful creation into a marketable product.

From Series A and onward, the startup has a solid product and the CEO is focused on scaling up the startup.

Marketing & the CEO

Marketing professionals will work closely with the startup CEO at the seed stage. At seed stage, the CEO will need an investor's slide deck and a powerful pitch for potential investors. Marketing may not attend these meetings, but marketing will be producing all of the content in preparation for the CEO's meetings with angel and seed investors. When the CEO asks you to join in on a meeting, even better. Let the CEO run the show and learn from the experience.

The CEO sets startup goals and targets and marketing is a part of this. Marketing professionals will be tasked with creating content and building the startup's marketing foundation at the seed stage. From Series A and onward, the CEO pushes marketing team members to deliver high quality leads at a fast pace.

Marketing & COO

Not every startup has a COO, a Chief Of Operations. The COO is responsible for operations, which touches every aspect of the startup. At the seed stage, the COO is also the acting CFO and "Deputy CEO". The COO is in charge of procuring materials that everyone needs, approving expenses and making payments to vendors. Even if there is an office manager, the COO is heavily involved in everything that goes in and out of the startup. When I refer to the COO also serving as "Deputy CEO", I mean that the CEO often gives the COO tasks to do – preparing for a meeting with investors, travel logistics, interviewing new candidates, closing a deal on office space and everything else that the business requires. At the seed and even Series A stage, there may not be a lot of people on the business side and the COO handles those tasks.

When the first sales are made and the first customers are ready to be the first to pay for your product, it is the COO's responsibility to successfully onboard the new customers. At this stage, there is no customer success team. Of course the VP Sales can participate in the first onboarding experiences, but it is up to the COO to put the people and processes into place and hit the finish line with customers who are actually benefiting from your product.

The COO views the world from the prism of the Excel spreadsheet. The interaction between marketing and the COO begins with the marketing budget. A budget is a plan of action with costs. Marketing and the COO should discuss goals and what it takes to reach them. Come up with a budget that works for both sides. The COO is most interested in the top level costs – campaigns, PR, website design – while marketing decides where and how to spend the money at the granular level.

As time passes and your startup grows, your goals and budget change. Coordinate these changes with the COO.

Marketing & VP Sales

The VP Sales is your most important partner – even more than the CEO. I love working with sales executives and have learned a lot from them. Sales professionals have the toughest job in any startup. They start every quarter at zero, are constantly rejected by people they speak with and are selling something that requires a lot of explaining.

It is absolutely vital that Marketing and Sales are aligned. The two teams need a solid funnel that both sides understand. Definitions must be clear – lead, marketing qualified lead, sales qualified lead, decision maker and influencer.

Plan weekly meetings with your sales team. Ask them these questions:

What is the hardest part of selling our product?
Who is the decision maker and who are the influencers?
What type of content helps to close the deal?
What content do you need that you don't currently have?
Are the CRM and marketing tools serving you well? If not, what can be done to improve how they help you?

Marketing serves sales. This is your number one priority.

It is often said that marketing professionals are farmers and sales professionals are hunters. Sales professionals themselves prefer to be called hunters. Marketing should also take on aspects of hunting. Create a Target List Spreadsheet. Speak with your sales team and come up with the top 100 companies that you want to sell to. Often a sales professional will be more than happy to work with marketing to create a Target List Spreadsheet.

Once you have the list, you can target those companies directly in LinkedIn via a paid campaign. LinkedIn lets you target companies by name. If the companies aren't too big, you can skip filtering and have the ads reach everyone. If the companies are too big, you can filter for job titles or whatever else you need in order to reach the right people.

Update your Target List Spreadsheet with your sales team as you progress.

In addition to online farming and hunting, marketing and sales work together in preparation for conferences. Months before a conference, the two sides should begin meeting to discuss logistics. Who does what and when. In the common scenario, marketing handles logistics and passes on assets to the sales team.

Find out what prints or other assets your VP Sales needs for the conference. Agree on goals for sales qualified leads and purchase orders within a 6-9 month timeline, depending on the length of your sales cycle. Typically, the entire sales team attends the conference while marketing stays home and works things behind the scenes. When marketing team members attend the conference, their role is to support sales efforts and manage the booth.

Marketing & VP Product

I enjoy working with startup sales teams because of the thrill of the hunt. I enjoy working with startup product teams because of the intellectual thrill. The VP Product and product team approach marketing when they are ready to turn a technology into a product. It begins with a datasheet. In some cases, marketing professionals will receive a draft datasheet to work on. If you're lucky, you will work on the product datasheet from the beginning with your product team.

This exercise in defining terms and phrases can be exciting. R&D and Product created an amazing thing, and now you get to express it in words. It takes a few sessions and many hours to create a datasheet for a complex technology product. The datasheet is the basis for all other content regarding the new product. Expect to work on many revisions.

Sometimes the product team needs marketing help for editing the words on a SaaS service. Without accurate communication and words on a service, no one will use it.

There are many other pieces of content that the startup product team will need to create with marketing's assistance. This includes product videos, white papers, webinars, press releases and blog posts. When you are writing product content, know when you need input from Product. After a few months, you should be able to produce the easy content (blog posts) without a lot of help from Product. Speaking of blog posts, it is a very good idea to have the VP Product and product team write their own blog posts that cover your product's best features.

The main event when Marketing and Product work together is for a new product release. A good product team will plan this months in advance and will give the marketing team a schedule of assets required and things-to-do. The product launch press release is (rightfully so) a big deal for Product. Product formulates the message and Marketing produces the content.

Marketing & VP R&D

Perhaps the longest distance in a startup is that between R&D and Marketing. R&D and Marketing may work together at the seed stage when there is no product team. In this scenario, R&D and Marketing join forces to do initial product marketing.

I was at a startup that had a VP R&D and didn't have a VP Product. It was a dangerous situation. The product was never fully fleshed out and there was no "check and balance" on R&D. There was no one to "fight" Android fragmentation and ensure that most features worked on popular Android devices. Product professionals are tough – they take mushy things and solidify them. Without them, technology products won't pass muster with the audience and no one will use it.

At another technology company that existed for over 10 years at the time, there was also no product team. The technology that R&D developed was amazing and yes, they successfully turned it into a real product. However, without a proper product development roadmap and standards, the company's product remains in a narrow niche with zero chance to breakout to other markets.

That said, without R&D there is no startup.

Marketing & CFO

Once a startup gets big enough, the role of CFO is separated from the COO. When a startup has over 100 employees, it will likely require a fulltime CFO. The CFO brings financial order to a startup. Marketing works with the CFO with regards to money – marketing budget and conferences.

Be organized! Create a folder for each vendor and save all bills, receipts and contracts in the corresponding folder.

When you begin preparations for a conference, speak with your CFO and establish a process for vendors and whatever other expenses you will have. Prepare the CFO for payments that will have to be made quickly and for whatever other challenges that might involve the financial side. Know how payments are made at your startup so you can tell vendors what to expect and when.

The worst scenario is when marketing is constantly running to finance to pay bills with a broken process. If it takes a meeting to smooth things out between the two sides, organize it and create a well-defined payments process.

CHAPTER 3

A Journey Through the Marketing-Sales Funnel

Throughout this book, I mention the Marketing-Sales Funnel. It is vital for the business side to have a deep understanding of the pipeline and how it functions. The CEO, COO, VP Marketing, VP Sales and even VP Product need to be 100% aligned. In this chapter, we will go on a journey through the Marketing-Sales Funnel and explore every aspect and how it affects startups.

Marketing-Sales Funnel in the Real World

A man walks into a clothing retailer. The minute he steps through the door, he has entered the store's Marketing-Sales Funnel. The pool of people who make purchases are located inside the store – not in the parking lot and not at home (no online purchases in this case).

Entering the store, he becomes a potential buyer. He is at the beginning of the store's Marketing-Sales Funnel.

Our male clothes shopper heads to the jeans rack. He picks up a pair of black jeans. Holding the jeans, he touches the material and makes note of the style. Next, he looks at the label and sees the price.

He is now in the middle of the funnel – he is looking at a product and considering quality, cost and suitability.

He asks a sales person a question and moves a step closer to the end of the store's Sales-Marketing Funnel.

Next, he goes into a dressing room and tries on the jeans. He looks in the mirror and decides he likes the jeans.

Now our guy is even closer to the end of the funnel – he entered the store, picked up a pair of jeans, asked a question and tried on the jeans. He is one step away from the funnel's finish line.

Finally, he walks up to the cash register and pays for the jeans. He walks out of the store with a branded bag and a smile.

He has completed the store's Marketing-Sales Funnel. Not only that, if he likes what he bought and had a pleasant experience at the store, he may return and buy more clothes.

Now let's change the item and add some complexity to our story. Instead of jeans, the guy is looking to buy a car.

He visits a car dealership and enters their Marketing-Sales Funnel.

He speaks with a sales person and goes on a test drive. This is the equivalent of trying on the jeans. But this time, he doesn't buy the car. He thanks the sales person and goes home. Even the sales person doesn't expect him to purchase a car on the first visit.

Why?

The more expensive the item, the more time we spend researching and deciding. While someone looking to buy a pair of jeans *may* not insist on visiting two stores to compare, someone buying a new car will almost definitely visit two or more car dealerships and check out the options.

The higher the price, the longer the funnel.

Consider how much you research buying things that cost $5, $100, $1,000 and $50,000.

In the case of the car, the car dealership has to collect the prospect's information and call him back. They will also hand out brochures so potential car buyers will consider their products while at home. The more "contact points" for car buyers, the better – phone calls, brochures, newspaper and TV ads to reinforce the message, sponsorships at local events and more.

Growing up in the 1980's, we received brochures and catalogs in the mail all the time. Some were hundreds of pages thick, others just a few pages. They did have an impact. We had no way to read more about products without leaving the house, so information was mailed to consumers. Sears and other companies were experts at sending relevant content to consumers a very long time ago.

Companies in the past would have given their eye tooth to allow consumers to read all about them from their home or pocket gadget. And when a sales representative wanted to speak with someone, that person had to be home, because almost no one had a mobile phone, until car phones began to gain traction.

It was even harder to be a consumer in the "old days". You could ask your friends for advice, but you had no way of reading reviews from people three time zones away. You collected information in person, on the phone, and by reading the small amount of content that was available.

Today, everything has changed, but the concepts remain the same. Let's take a look at the Online Marketing-Sales Funnel.

Marketing-Sales Funnel in the Online World

Twenty years later, our jeans guy is back at it again. He's looking for a pair of black jeans, same waist size as before. He can go to a brick and mortar store, but decides to buy the jeans online. Instead of visiting a retailer, he heads straight to the jeans brand's website.

He types in the URL and the page loads.

Our jeans guy is now at the beginning of the online store's Marketing-Sales Funnel.

He views a few products and moves himself along the funnel. There is no sales representative, but he can chat live with someone if he chooses. He likes the hi-res closeups of the jeans. The content is informative and concise.

He adds a pair of jeans to his shopping cart and moves closer to the end of the funnel. At this point, he can "leave the store" by closing the tab. He can leave the tab open and "stay in the store". But our guy is persistent – he goes to the online cash register and pays for the jeans.

He has reached the end of the funnel.

By visiting the store's website, he receives a cookie on his browser. For the next few months, he will be bombarded with ads. He may or may not return to purchase more clothes, but he won't be lacking in reminders! No one has to physically mail him a catalog. He can view an updated version anytime he wants.

His email address is added to the store's email list. They will email him a few times a year (or more) to try to entice him to make more purchases.

In his free time, he can read reviews about jeans and other clothing items. He has many great options for reading online reviews, but he is wisely skeptical of their accuracy and source.

Now, let's exchange the jeans for a new car yet again.

Our guy decides to buy a car. Before spending tens of thousands of dollars, he reads a ton of content for 3-6 months. He visits the car manufacturers' websites, auto magazines and news, review sites and everything he can find on the first 10 pages of Google search results.

He isn't going to buy the car online, per se, but he is educating himself without taking up direct time of a sales person. Yes, the automobile marketing teams are creating and distributing content, but they don't interact directly with the prospect.

By the time he visits a local car dealership, he has invested dozens of hours over a period of 3-6 months in learning about his wants, needs and which car model best suits him. He visits a few local car dealerships and test drives a few cars. Finally, he makes a second visit to one of the car dealerships and signs on the dotted line.

Yes, the sales person from the car dealership called our guy and tried to entice him to return. But our guy was able to do his research from the comfort of his home, reading through massive amounts of car related content.

Thanks to online marketing, he is able to move his way to the end of the Marketing-Sales Funnel on his own, with little direct interaction with the car dealership.

In this last example, our guy decides to buy a new laptop. He quickly puts together what he needs – a top rated i7 Ultrabook. He reads content for a few weeks and makes the purchase online. In this case, there isn't even a visit to a brick and mortar store.

In the online world, marketing is responsible for offering potential customers all of the "touch points" so they can make a purchase. This is the case for both B2B and B2C. The content is offered in two areas – website and everywhere else. You control the content on your website, and do your best to shape the content that others create about your brand.

The Three Stages of the Sales-Marketing Funnel

There are three stages to the Sales-Marketing Funnel. Beginning, middle and end. You need to create content and a story for all three stages.

Let's go back to our jeans guy who also bought a car.

When he enters the store (online or offline), he is at the beginning of the funnel.

When he looks at a product or asks a question, he is in the middle of the funnel.

When he adds an item to his shopping cart, he is at the end of the funnel.

Your blog posts, home page and product pages provide content for the beginning of the funnel. It gets them inside.

Deeper content, such as, "Tips on getting the most out of your ..." is middle of the funnel content.

"Our product vs the competition" is an example of end of the funnel content. This is when they have read a number of pieces of content about your product, and are comparing you to the competition. This is the make it or break it moment – a company has to be able to capture end of the funnel prospects.

You also have to get them into your funnel in the first place, and move them along the stages. The first two stages are "farming", while getting potential customers through the end of the funnel and paying for your product is always going to be a challenge.

It is one thing to browse an item, and another to pay for it.

Marketing-Sales Funnel Recommendations

Segment your funnel and prepare marketing and sales for each stage. Who does what and when? The obvious first step is to create the initial content for the beginning stage of the funnel – your website, blog, press releases and campaigns to introduce people to your funnel.

What is your optimal middle of the funnel content? Create a lot – cover all of your bases. Your customers have different needs and past experiences. Make it visually easy to learn more and reach out to your side.

How do you close the deal? Is it done 100% online? It is like the car scenario where it begins online and ends in a real world business meeting? Does it end with a phone call to the potential customer? Are marketing and sales on the same page as far as goals? Is marketing listening to and serving sales?

When you create campaigns, target all three stages of the funnel. Retargetting is how you target those who are in the middle or end of your funnel. We all experience retargeted ads. The content of retargetting banners and landing pages should reflect the stage.

The people who have visited your website probably know what you sell. Move them along the funnel with testimonials, case studies and media articles and mentions to reinforce the message that your company is the one to buy from. Move from "Who we are" to "Why we're good". Hit hard on your powerful features.

Campaigns which bring new potential customers into the funnel should consider the needs and pains of the person who may buy your product. Talk to their needs. They don't care what awards you've won. Show them quality and value. The most important thing to get right is to learn how to successfully communicate with your audience.

When you analyze leads through the funnel, identify their stage and figure our where your weak point is. Find a winning strategy for that stage of the funnel and pounce on it! Visualize your startup's Marketing-Sales Funnel every single day.

CHAPTER 4

Decision Makers and Influencers

A startup is a business. Every business has a pool of potential customers who are most likely to need your products and services. Let's begin at home.

Decision Making at Home

Who decides where to buy food and what food to buy? Are you the decision maker or is it your partner? If you are not the decision maker, are you the influencer who suggests what food to buy, but doesn't make the final decision? As an influencer, maybe you just pay for the food and don't get involved in logistics. It could be that the two of you are decision makers. Maybe you are the decision maker on the cookies and your partner is the decision maker on everything else.

Now consider who makes decisions on buying more expensive items, such as refrigerators, washing machines and televisions. If one of you knows a lot about an appliance, you will likely be the decision maker and your partner will be the influencer. If your partner is an audiophile, he or she will likely be the decision maker when it comes to buying a new stereo or soundbar, and you will be the influencer.

In many cases, there is a decision maker and no influencer. Maybe your partner decides on the food and you don't get involved. Perhaps you are the red wine decision maker and your partner isn't even an influencer.

In a home with children, there may be many influencers when it comes to food. There are many parenting books about not allowing your children to become decision makers!

Decision Making Process at Home

Now that we know who decides what, we can discuss how they reach their decisions. Let's begin with the inexpensive stuff. What goes into your or your partner's decision on what bread to buy? Is there a particular type of bread you prefer? Is health a consideration? Do you buy a few types of breads and rolls in order to make everyone happy? As bread is a lot less expensive than a new washing machine, you can make a spur of the moment decision to try a different type of bread without researching it.

Let's up our game. This time, you need a new microwave which will cost $50-$200. A lot more than a loaf of bread, but a lot less than a new refrigerator or bedroom set. The decision maker will probably want to read about microwaves online and learn about cooking features, size considerations and respected brands. A few articles and a few conversations. The decision making process can be measured in hours or days for a microwave.

Finally, you and your partner reach the top of the mountain and decide to buy a new car. A car will cost tens of thousands of dollars and there are a multitude of things to consider. Who will drive it? What type of car do you need? What colors and styles do you prefer? What is your spending limit? What new car features do you need?

Both the decision maker and influencer will read articles online, visit car dealerships and go on test drives. The process for buying a new car is a lot longer than the process for buying a hamburger roll. 3-6 months is a realistic range for covering every step of the decision making process.

Decision Making Process For Startups

At a startup, the CEO, VP Marketing and VP Sales should have in-depth discussions on decision makers and influencers. For a product on the shelves for decades, the seller knows who the decision makers and influencers are. When you have a "revolutionary game changing product" on your hands, you can't rely on the past.

The founders of a startup knew of a need for the technology that they developed. Next the product team took the reins and created something that real people can actually use. Using something and selling something are two different things. The CEO, Sales and Marketing need to learn everything they can about the decision making process for their specific product and industry.

B2B Decision Makers & Influencers

Let's take a look at decision makers, influencers and the process for a B2B startup. B2B startups typically sell products and services that cost tens of thousands to hundreds of thousands of dollars. 5 to 6 digits is a big deal. Of course there are B2B startups selling products for millions of dollars.

The people buying these 5-6 digit products that startups sell are mid to high level professionals who make upper 5 to 6 digital salaries. They are very experienced and most have been decision makers or influencers for decades. They know how to formulate a decision making process and are loyal to their company's needs.

Marketing schtick won't cut it.

Decision makers and influencers are likely avid readers of the tools used in their field. They are seeking quality information about ways to improve their organization's situation (revenues or productivity in most cases).

When your startup has a meeting or series of meetings regarding decision makers and influencers, discuss these questions:

Who are the people who are authorized to make decisions to buy your product?

What industry/industries do your decision makers and influencers work in?

What are the most common job titles of your decision makers and influencers?

What department do your decision makers and influencers work in?

Who is the final decision maker – the one who signs off on the purchase?

Will you need to persuade both technical professionals and business professionals?

Are the technical professionals the "first step in the door" and are the business professionals the ones who sign off on the purchase?

Is your product so expensive that it requires the CFO or CEO to approve purchasing?

What size companies do your typical decision makers and influencers work in? Small and medium sized businesses or large corporations?

Is there a difference in how you would target decision makers and influencers at small businesses and those at large corporations?

What product features are a hit with each type of decision maker and influencer?

What are the biggest concerns that your decision makers and influencers have regarding your product?

What is the most common factor that holds up closing a deal? Is it a product issue, corporate culture on the other side or something else entirely?

From past experience with sales (if you have this luxury), which decision makers and influencers participated in the fastest lead-to-purchase-order from your funnel? Look at your previous sales and analyze the "crime scene" and try to identify people and actions which accelerated the sales process.

Map it all out. Create a document and get everyone in Sales and Marketing fully aligned. Update it as your product or market undergo changes.

Feed Your Decision Makers

Now that you know all there is to know about your decision makers and influencers, your next goal is to "feed them with content". Create a large list of content that your decision makers and influencers are interested in.

Consider the 3 stages that people pass through while on the way to completing a purchase:

1. We read about the topic
2. We read about the challenges and pains involved in the topic
3. We read about solutions to the challenges

Stage 1 content should cover your industry/field/topic

Stage 2 content should cover the challenges and pains – often in the form of tips and best practices

Stage 3 content should cover your solution vs the competition and your solution's most attractive features

Now, create every type of content for all 3 stages! This includes blog posts, eBooks, top level content pages that appear on your top menu bar, press releases, thought leadership articles published on news and industry websites, datasheets, text and visual comparisons, illustrations, interactive content such as ROI calculators and anything else you can come up with that makes your case.

In short, discover who your decision makers and influencers are and give them everything they need in order to complete a journey through your funnel.

B2C Decision Makers & Influencers

Selling to consumers is a very different game than selling to businesses. If you are a B2C startup, you begin with the same thing as the B2B startup – a meeting.

Unlike B2B, in B2C, marketing owns the funnel. There may be a VP Sales and a sales function – especially in startups that sell expensive products to consumers (think cars, appliances and high-end gadgets and tools). But in most cases, B2C marketing professionals are responsible for taking leads from beginning to end (sale).

Consider these points as you map out your decision makers and influencers for a B2C startup:

Who buys your product?

Is there a geographical base or areas where your product sells better than in other areas of the world?

What role does gender play?

What situation leads people to decide they need your product?

Segment your decision makers with as much detail as you can – geography, gender (if relevant), age range and income levels.

Determine where your target audience spends their time online. Every demographic has different preferences when it comes to social media, news and leisure. Some different demographics will reveal similar habits (like Facebook or Instagram) and some will involve a niche (people who are interested in automobile technologies or fashion).

For B2C, your product is likely either useful, entertaining or both. For a less expensive product, there won't be all the 3 well-defined stages of the funnel journey. In fact, for most B2C products, all 3 stages are merged into one stage.

You can imagine one piece of content containing all 3 stages – about your (hopefully) cool industry padded with useful information and closing with why your product is best. A lot easier to do for a pair of jeans than for an ERP tool.

For B2C, you can usually afford to be more creative and out-of-the-box as opposed to conservative B2B marketing. The same B2B director who expects a regal tone to your B2B brand may be a very different person at home! Travel and fashion tech startups should create colorful, fun to read content for their audiences. The content you create can read more like a Rolling Stone article than a quarterly report. Of course this all depends on your brand.

Create content that goes viral. When you create the perfect content, your audience will help you to distribute the content. Viral content distribution is very efficient. Talk to your audience's needs and wants, add some charm, wit and color to your content and watch it go viral. Determine the red lines – things you won't do, because they may harm the brand. Keep it positive.

CHAPTER 5

A Startup's First Website

Startups don't have physical stores. You won't find them at the mall. Your website is the focal point for your audience's first impression of your brand. For early stage startups who aren't yet participating in conferences, your website is the only source for people to find you. Even if you are listed in Crunchbase and have made appearances in the media, your website is where the game is at.

The good news is that you have 100% control over your website. Building a website should be one of the first major projects for a startup upon reaching the end of the prototype stage and heading for product. You may avoid a website while in stealth mode – or put together a quick 3-5 page mini-site for stealth mode. When you can see the finish line with your first "ready for sale" product, it is time to produce your startup's website.

Your first website is important because it sets the stage for the future. You need a CMS – a content management system. I call them "content engines" – a platform to add and edit content for your website. There are literally hundreds today. The three major CMS's are:

- WordPress
- Joomla
- Drupal

Drupal was first released in 2001, Joomla in 2005 and WordPress in 2003.

On the ease of use scale, WordPress is easiest, followed by Joomla and finally Drupal. Web developers consider Joomla and Drupal to be more advanced – and they are, if you are enterprise. For a small startup looking to "hit the airwaves" quickly and quietly, WordPress is the best option.

Here's how it works:

All 3 CMS's are free. There are themes and plugins which cost money. A few hundred dollars will go a long way when buying your first startup theme and a few vital plugins.

Installation is easy – anyone with minimal web development knowledge can install an instance of WordPress.

Here is a quick step-by-step guide to create your startup's first website. The goal is to be quick and practical. Build your foundation and move onto greater things.

Step 1 - Find a Web Developer

You will need a web developer, unless a member of your team happens to have good web development knowledge. You are not doing custom programming, you are installing an instance of WordPress (or whatever CMS you choose), customizing it and ensuring that the website serves your startup's needs as far as content, branding and lead generation.

After your initial launch, you will need your web developers for additions to the site, but not for adding blog posts and news items. Marketing should take care of that. WordPress is easy enough for non-technical people to upload new content. You will need web developers perhaps when you make style changes to product and technology pages or add new features.

As a minor step, you need a web host. Consult with your web developers. I've used GoDaddy and Rackspace, and there are hundreds more.

There are even web hosts that specialize in WordPress hosting, and can offer special features – like development and production servers. This allows you to work on a non-live version of your website, and move the content to a live server once you have tested all changes. Just like R&D.

Step 2 – Find a Graphics Designer

Design is just as important as content. Find a graphics designer who is experienced with startup websites. He or she will help you to lay the foundation for the visual aspect of your brand. This is so important to get right the first time!

Step 3 – A Website Summit

Now it's time to make decisions. The bottom line – what pages will your startup website contain? Marketing should run this project while getting input – and approval – from the CEO, VP Product and other principals.

Start off with "Who are we?" Spend a few hours discussing who you are and how you want to portray yourself. A lot of this depends on who your sales targets will be. Think ahead! Eventually you will need to entice real people to buy your product. Yes, you want to impress potential investors and technology journalists, but keep your eye on the ball and create a brand that your target audience will instantly connect with.

Create a logo and decide on the two main colors for the menu and web pages. Make a list of web pages to be created for initial launch. Here is a template of what pages your startup may need:

- Home
- About Us
- Management
- Contact Us
- Product Pages

- Technology Pages
- Video
- Blog
- News

You should end up with 15-20 pages. Remember, you can always add more content and features later. My experience with startup CEO's is they prefer fast over comprehensive when it comes to the first version of the startup's website. No startup CEO will ever give you 6 months to produce a "perfect website". You will get 2-3 months if you're lucky, and 1 month if you're not.

During your "Website Summit" – which will probably take place over a few meetings, consider these points:

What special website features do you want to launch with? Customizing WordPress isn't expensive, and even if it requires 10-20 hours of work to add something interactive to your website, it may be worth it.

Do you have a video? Nearly every startup has a short 30 seconds to two minutes video that is their elevator pitch to the world. Yes, you can launch your website and produce a video as the next project.

Choose a CRM if you will be generating leads. Salesforce is the biggest name in the business, but I recommend starting off with a smaller, easier to use CRM at first. For time's sake more than money. If your needs are "web form to CRM", start off with a basic CRM that will cost $0 to $100 a month and will run itself once properly installed.

Where do you want the lead gen / Get A Demo / Contact Us forms? On every page? On every blog post as well? I say yes to all of the above – you want to be capable of capturing leads or contacts from every page on your site.

What plugins will you start off with? There are many useful WordPress plugins that you want to consider using. There are terrific SEO plugins which ensure that your website is SEO friendly. It may be that the free version of an SEO plugin is good enough to start with. How about a backup plugin that downloads an archive of your website every so often. I recommend weekly website backups – unless you're making hourly changes to your website, that will do it. Be a pro and regularly copy your website backup to other locations on and off of your network. A typical WordPress backup archive is a few hundred GB's of data – not a lot.

There are plugins for everything under the sun:

- Add a map to your Contact Us page
- eCommerce
- Compressing photos so your site is optimized
- Contact forms
- Google Analytics
- Connecting your website to other services that you use, such as a CRM or marketing automation tools.

Step 4 – Write the Content

Now that you know the names of the pages that you need to create, it is time to start writing! Start with the easy part – Contact Us, About Us and move onto the harder pages – Product and Technology. Make sure all relevant parties sign off and approve on the pages that cover their expertise. The VP Product is your partner when it comes to website content creation. He or she built the product and it is up to the two of you to translate the product into quality content.

Step 5 – Add Design

Now you have words, but zero design. Bring in your graphics designer and have them add design to the page. What you end up with is exactly what you will be giving the web developers to implement. Your designer will likely need to buy stock photos as well as work on some original graphics.

The big decision here is what theme to use – or will you design your own. You can take an existing WordPress or CMS theme and customize it. Whatever you do, keep an eye on the clock – you can't afford to spend months on perfecting design.

When you are dealing with a complex technology, you need a few powerful images that depict your solution. This is often the toughest part of the design. One trick is to take existing stock photos and have your designer customize them – adding whatever it is you do to the stock photo.

For example, if your startup does something with transportation, smartphones, IoT or anything – find the photos that are the "basis" of what you do, and have a designer "add your magic/technology" to the photos.

Step 6 – Development Site

Your web pages are now ready to be "turned into WordPress". Bring in the web developers. Have them add whatever "special features" that you specify. The site should be viewable by your team, but not open to the world. It is not live.

Edit, make changes, improve, fine-tune it and do your best to bring this process to an end.

Step 7 – Turn on the Lights and Go Live!

When you are ready, tell your web developers to "Go live!"

Congratulations – your startup is no longer in stealth mode and the world – and hopefully success – awaits you.

After going live, expect the unexpected. Have everyone on the team QA the site. Better to find and resolve issues during the first week than later on. Keep the development site if you have one, so you can test any changes offline. Even changing a headline can sometimes cause problems with a theme. As much as you want to be hands-on and get things done quickly, be aware than any changes that you make yourself can affect the website. Unless you know what you're doing, let the web developers make top level content changes (i.e., everything besides the updated content – like the blog and news, which marketing should handle).

Step 8 – Continue to Add Content

You thought you were done?! You should be updating your website 1-3 times a week! When you have something to say, let Google – and the world – know. Here are examples of what you will be updating on your startup's website. In the Content chapter, I discuss these in much more detail:

- Blog Posts – weekly is a good standard to start with. If you add 2-3 blog posts a month at first, that's fine.
- News – the news section on your website is the perfect place for short blurbs. Media appearances, conferences attended, new product launches and partnerships. Your blog can have full articles on these topics, while the news section has a short version.
- New Products and Services
- Homepage – you will always update your homepage to reflect "the big thing" going on at your startup.

Continue to work with your designer and web developers on customizing your site. Decide the pace – even a small $5k a quarter budget will go a long way. The more you can allocate to your website, the more complex features you can add. On the other hand, avoid being in a constant website update cycle if it doesn't add to your bottom line.

Your website should serve you and not the other way around!

CHAPTER 6

The Marketing Budget

The marketing department is often one of the biggest parts of a startup's expenses. At a certain point, more may be spent on marketing than R&D. Once R&D has the technology in place and the tools needed to develop it, the major cost is in people – the R&D team. When it comes to marketing, not only do you have a team of 1-5 people, they are all spending a lot of money on marketing tools, services and campaigns.

The marketing budget serves as a marketing activities dashboard. It lets you see how much you are spending. Every quarter and every year, compare the "in" number (expenses) with the "out" number (sales qualified leads and sales). Divide the two and you have a per lead ratio.

Before your CEO gives you money to spend, you will need to create a marketing budget.

Asset Allocation

Asset allocation is a very important term and tool from the world of investing. Let's say an investor has $100,000 cash that he wants to invest. He sets goals – a mix of low risk investments that grow slowly but surely with a sprinkling of high risk investments that he can afford to lose if they don't pan out.

The investment plan may look like this:

US Treasury Bills – 40%
S&P 500 Index Fund – 50%
Technology and Energy – 10%

Investing in Treasury Bills is low risk with a lower but steady pay-out of 1-3%. The S&P 500 grows by an average annual return of 9.8%. This fluctuates year by year. There is much higher risk in that some years, the S&P 500 drops by 30% and sometimes it grows by 30%. Investors who have time can wait out the tough periods and see huge gains. Investors who don't have time get crushed.

Finally, the technology and energy investment is the biggest risk. How many current technology companies will be around in 30 years? How many will be around even in 10 years? The investment in technology and energy stocks can bring huge returns. According to CNBC, a $1,000 investment in Apple in 1980 would have been worth over $228,000 in 2016. Better yet, a $1,000 investment in Microsoft would have been worth $546,000 in 2016.

On the other hand, these companies could have flopped and your $1,000 would have been worth $0.

Asset Allocation & Startup Marketing

Learning investment asset allocation is a great way to gain a better understanding of the marketing budget. There are differences – your marketing budget won't automatically grow based on good results and you don't have a 30-year timeframe for success.

Consider what % of your budget you will allocate for everything you need –

Content and Design – What % of your budget should go to content and design?

Marketing Tools – What % of your budget should be allocated to marketing tools?

Campaigns – Make sure you are spending enough here as campaigns are your primary source for lead generation.

Marketing Budget Components

There are many possible components to a startup marketing budget. In this section, I will offer a big picture selection of marketing budget components. Consider these and whatever other special needs and costs you might have.

Conferences – The first item to knock off. If you are going to be hosting a booth at a conference, you will likely be spending $50-$70k (or more) per conference. Even if you are just sending a few people and doing a few things, put the conference component on top so it doesn't get mixed in with everything else.

Public Relations – Next is your PR agency retainer and costs.

Content and Design – Content and graphics design go hand-in-hand. Many pieces of content require design. Some of your design costs may be allocated either here or in the conference section where applicable.

Web Developers – What is your monthly or quarterly cost for web development?

Online Campaigns – The meat and potatoes of your startup marketing budget. Split this section into channels and track the costs of each channel, such as AdWords, LinkedIn and Facebook.

Marketing Tools – Your CRM, email and marketing automation tools go here.

Translations – Some startups translate every new top level content page into a few other languages, based on their sales targets.

Videos – Are you producing a video? If you plan on creating a proper product video, this should be added to your budget.

Vendors – Who else do you work with? If you pay a marketing vendor to help you with campaigns and other activities, create this section for your budget.

Everything Else – Every startup has its own specific marketing needs. They change over time. Add a section for "miscellaneous" with a few hundred dollars a month so you have room for surprises and don't have to play a game of asset allocation every time a new marketing expenditure emerges.

Final Notes on the
Startup Marketing Budget

The startup marketing budget is a work in progress. You may find yourself updating it weekly. It is a juggling act – you have a large list of things you need. Every wheel needs to turn in order for you to generate quality leads. Be ready to lower the budget of under-performing activities and move those funds to better sources of leads.

At first, you will spend a lot of resources on content creation and graphics design. You need to create a brand before you can market it. You need a website with dozens of pages of quality content before you can start running campaigns on LinkedIn.

Be thrifty. If the summer is a quiet season for your industry, lower your costs during the summer so you have more money when the business season opens in September. You can scale down campaigns and press releases a bit in the summer and spend more on content and design. Hit the ground running every September with tons of content and double down on campaigns during the fall and winter.

Finally, prepare yourself for surprises. Startup marketing budgets can be axed entirely for a quarter as your startup awaits an investment. Your CEO may ask you to stop all campaigns but continue to fund other activities. Or you may be asked to cut campaigns by a large percent. A week later, your budget can triple in size. If you find yourself managing a stable marketing budget, enjoy the short respite from startup chaos.

CHAPTER 7

Essential Marketing Tools

"Under the hood" of every startup website are marketing tools which allow you to track visitors, generate leads and even determine what content website visitors see. Other tools allow visitors to chat live with one of your representatives while others increase ecommerce conversions. There are tons of tools out there.

My goal in this chapter is to describe the vital tools that every startup website should have as well as a few amazing website marketing tools that you should know about. Over time, they change, but the basics of what they do is what you need to know.

Meet Google Analytics

Back in the early days of the internet, if you wanted to track your traffic, you had to pay a company $500-$1,000 a month. Then came Google Analytics, a free tool, which ate those companies alive. Nearly every serious website uses Google Analytics to track their website visitors. It does this and much more!

Imagine if a store was able to track:

Who entered the store (the funnel entry point)

Who picked up a product or asked a question to a sales person (the next step of the funnel – they are interacting and showing interest)

Who went to the cash register and paid

Who didn't buy anything at the store, but returned later to look again. Imagine if stores you visited in the real world were able to give you a personal cookie that personalizes ads that you see during your day.

A complete breakdown of the funnel numbers – from store visitors to what every visitor looked at to sales.

That's what Google Analytics does for your website!

When you sign up for Google Analytics (again, it is free) and verify that you own (or can make changes to) your startup's website, you are given a small piece of code that you have your web developers add to the website. They will know what to do with it – typically it goes in the header or footer.

Once Google Analytics tracking is live, you have a wealth of information at your fingertips. For starters, you will see how many website visitors you get per day, where they are from, what pages they visited, the most common entry and exit pages and of course the most common paths your visitors took while on your startup website.

You can break visitors down by operating system, country, language and much more.

Google Analytics Goal Completions

Let's say you have a form on your website – the classic Get A Demo form that many startups use. On this form, you are often asking people for their name, email address, country and perhaps a question related to your product or technology.

You want to be able to track how many people fill out the form. Google Analytics calls this a "Goal Completion".

Here is how it works:

When someone fills out a Get A Demo (or whatever you have) form on your website, they are taken to a "Thank You Page" which lets them know you received their request and that you will get back to them shortly (or whatever your message is). You've seen this many times.

On Google Analytics, when you create a Goal Completion, you tell Google Analytics what the "Thank You Page" URL is. The only way to reach the "Thank You Page" is by filling out your form.

Magic – now you know not only who visited your website, but who took the next step and filled out a form. The people who fill out forms are the "middle of the funnel" – they are reaching out for a demo, a sales person or more information.

There is one more vital step required in completing your startup's marketing-sales funnel – the CRM.

Your Startup's First CRM

When you connect Google Analytics to your WordPress website, you can have your web developers set it so certain people on your team receive emails every time a form is filled out. That's nice. But it's not enough.

A B2B startup needs a CRM in order to track these leads and have sales reach out to them. A CRM basically collects these leads and lets you view them, sort them, and even send emails to them. Sales professionals use the CRM to reach out to new and existing leads. The CEO and COO – and everyone who needs to – can see and track marketing and sales results in real time.

If you are a small startup, choose one of the many small CRM's. You can often have your web developers take care of connecting your lead generation form to your CRM. Consider what dashboards you need and customize it enough to keep you going for the first year.

Keep in mind that most early stage startups don't have the luxury of a CRM expert on-hand. You want your CRM to work seamlessly with zero or little maintenance required. If you grow too fast, you can always move to Salesforce or a more complex CRM.

A word to the wise – connecting a form, Google Analytics and a CRM is complex stuff. Test it multiple times – by filling out the form, skipping a field, and trying all sorts of possibilities and scenarios. If your form doesn't work, "the lights are out" on your startup.

One of the most exciting aspects of startup marketing is the moment the website goes live and leads start to flow in. It is a wonderful feeling to see that the funnel you built is working and is generating leads. The CRM results tab is hard to close, even at night! And when paid campaigns start to kick in, these numbers can grow exponentially.

Determine Lead Flow

Lead flow can get very complicated. I've seen many technology companies make it even more complicated than it needed to be. The result? Too much time was spent on fixing processes and editing documents no one will read, and too little time was spent on lead generation marketing activities. Nonetheless, you need to determine a clear flow of leads. Who gets them and what happens at every stage of the game.

In this scenario, a startup has a Get A Demo form on their website.

A website visitor fills out a form. Google Analytics tracks it as a Goal Completion and the lead appears in the CRM.

Who receives an automatic email with the lead info? In a small startup, this may be the CEO, VP Marketing, VP Sales and perhaps VP

Product. There is no issue with more people receiving these emails, but the responsibility for what happens should involve a very small number of people.

Now that a bunch of you have received an email, what happens? In most cases, Sales calls the lead, and if the lead is from a country you don't work with, Sales emails the lead. Whatever the case, make concrete decisions.

What is a Marketing Qualified Lead? Is it any person who fills out a Get A Demo form? Or just people from certain countries or from specific industries? The idea is to create a definition that answers this question – "Is the lead someone who Sales *could* sell our product to?" If the answer is yes, then you have a Marketing Qualified Lead.

Sales speaks with the lead and either qualifies or doesn't qualify the Marketing Qualified Lead. If qualified, a demo is scheduled. Who takes the baton from here? It could be the same sales professional or a demo call with Sales and Product. Decide.

A demo call has taken place and is successful. Who puts together the sale? Who is involved, and who has full responsibility?

What happens when Sales speaks to leads and they aren't ready to buy? Are emails sent to them every month? Do they receive another sales call? If a sales professional makes a note in the CRM to call the lead at a later date, is this tracked and by whom?

You can read the above and fill in the blanks for your own startup based on your needs. Create a lead flow document, answer all of these questions. The bottom line is to avoid losing good leads.

The Hardest Part of a New CRM – Culture!

Now that you have Google Analytics and a CRM for your website, you are ready for the hardest part when it comes to a new CRM – changing your startup's culture!

A CRM is worthless if no one looks at it. Your CEO, COO, VP Sales and VP Marketing need to "want" to use it. Most experienced CEO's are very comfortable using a CRM and will give you great ideas for customizing the dashboard and information flow. Listen to them. The same goes with your VP Sales. Your VP Sales is in the jungle, fighting one quarter at a time. At a good startup, you will learn a lot about improving lead flow from your CEO and VP Sales.

When the CRM goes live, offer a CRM Workshop – in person or via video conferencing if some of you are remote. Spend an hour giving everyone a tour. Send everyone a login so they can experience it themselves. Skip the PowerPoint presentation and have someone fill out a form, and have everyone reload the CRM's leads page so they see it. Explain it as a lead flow process as opposed to just a technical process.

I enjoy these "CRM conversations". The R&D people who join in are often shocked that marketing is so technical.

If you have the best CRM configuration in the world, and it is too complex for your team to use, you will need to work at it to make sure that your CRM serves your startup. Be patient! Most of your team members have never used the CRM you chose. **Get Sales onboard, and it will be a lot easier to change the culture of your startup to that of "we have an amazing idea" to "we have an amazing idea that is making millions of dollars".**

Beyond The CRM – Marketing Automation

Google Analytics and the CRM are the first step. Beyond, there is a plethora of marketing tools out there. I want to discuss them – not for their specs, but in order to give readers a sense of the powerful capabilities that can be added to your startup.

If you are reading this book, then you know what email marketing is. Leads from your CRM can be sent emails. Wonderful. In the classic scenario, this is done manually, and without filtering who gets what. If you want, you can filter email blasts manually by exporting leads to Excel and creating different groups of leads in your email tool (whether you use your CRM's email marketing or an outside tool).

Then, you can send emails manually every so often. Oh, you will need to manually update these lists with new leads. I had to do this at one technology company, and on "Email day", I spent half the day just preparing to send the emails.

At another company, we used Marketo. What a world of difference. Recall the manual scenario we just discussed and let's see what Marketo, Hubspot or any of the many excellent marketing automation tools can do for you.

With marketing automation, new leads are automatically entered not only to the CRM but also to email lists. You can determine the filtering and groups by your own specific needs. For examples, leads can be separated into email groups based on country, region, industry, title or anything on your website form.

Better yet, you can create "new paths" for leads to experience on the way to the finish line (when they become a Marketing Qualified Lead and the hand-off from Marketing to Sales takes place). Imagine your startup sells a complex product - so complex that filling out a form isn't enough in most cases in order to offer a demo. You want them to experience more of your website before they get the call. The more expensive your product, the more likely you will want to implement scoring.

When a website visitor fills out a form, they get a tracking cookie. Every action they do gives them points – that you determine. For example:

- Read a blog post – 10 points
- Read a datasheet – 30 points
- Attend a webinar – 60 points
- Read a product page – 20 points
- Fill out a form – 50 points
- Read an email – 20 points

Let's say the requisite score for a call from Sales is 100 points. When that happens, you can decide who receives an email. Any action can trigger an email.

Even if your startup doesn't require a score for a Sales call, it is very useful for a sales professional speaking to a lead to know what activities they have taken on the website. The more you know about what your leads do on your property, the more you will sell.

Stage 1, 2 and 3

You want to offer your website visitors multiple paths to become leads. Create a series of emails that you send to leads.

A Stage 1 email is "about the topic" that your product or technology covers. You can offer a PDF eBook to read, a blog post – anything involving a call to action and a link.

Those who click on the link are added to the Stage 2 Email Group. The Stage 2 Email Group receives an email that is "about the challenges and pains" that your product resolves. Same process – offer a link to content.

Those who click on the Stage 2 Email are added to the Stage 3 Email Group. This group receives an email "about your cure to the problem" – why it is vital/needed.

Those who click on the Stage 3 Email are ready to speak with Sales.

Think of it this way –

Stage 1 is "Winter is coming, I'm interested in reading about how to avoid the flu and other winter health issues."

Or

"I am starting to look for a new car. I'm not sure what car I want to buy, but I am beginning my journey and will read a lot before I contact a dealer."

Stage 2 is "How the flu can harm you."

Or

"I am starting to realize my needs when it comes to buying a new car. What pitfalls should I avoid and what killer info can I learn?"

Stage 3 is "I am actively looking for a solution to the flu. I think I need to get a flu shot and buy cold medicine."

Or

"I have determined my needs and am actively looking to buy a car. I have a few models in mind and will reach out to relevant car dealers."

During this process, the lead is checking you out. He or she is exposed to your brand, your website, your communication. You can make it or break it with a pleasant, informative and automatic process.

When the above scenario is running smoothly, you massively grow your lead generation potential. Not only are things automatic, but sales professionals are empowered by knowing much more about the lead's activities and interests. This is good for both the lead and your startup.

As a consumer, I realize I am being tracked. I know when I visit a website that I will see their ads for the next few weeks (or years in the worst cases!). I decide when to click, when to reply, when to respond. Most of the time I don't, but when I do, I feel I have done my research and am ready to make an inquiry or purchase. All of the content that I read along the way prepared me for my decision – whether it is a car, a smartphone, or clothes.

Scale Your Way to the Top

There is so much more that marketing automation can do for a startup. The key is to scale up at the right pace. Even if you have an unlimited budget, every new complex marketing automation tool will require a lot of time to implement, and there is a long learning curve. For the first stage of your marketing activities, you want to begin with a small selection of tools and scale up accordingly. When you are making $1 million a year or more in sales, consider upgrading your CRM and look into new marketing automation tools.

It is more important to get your basics right at first than to be able to say you have every major marketing automation tool up and running. Perfect your messaging, campaign strategies and tactics, develop the content of your website.

Social Media Posting Tools

When your marketing is at the point where you are doing multiple social media posts per week on a few channels, consider a social media tool. Social media tools optimize and automate social media posts. Why login to Facebook, LinkedIn and Twitter and manually post your message when you can use a tool that lets you enter in your content, decide where to post it, and even how often.

Good social media posting tools help you to decide when to post – there is a whole science on this. Your audience is all over the world and timing matters.

There is one other amazing thing that a good social media posting tool can do – your team members can login once to the tool, and subsequent posts can be done not only from the company page, but by their profiles as well. The R&D team may be less interested in this, but it is good to have posts come not only from your company's voice, but from your product, sales and marketing teams.

Social media is a world – and profession – unto itself. Many young marketing professions get their start with social media. Social media is always evolving. Consider these tips when setting your social media marketing goals:

A presence on social media will help your SEO efforts. If you are a B2B startup, you may be correct in not running massive Facebook campaigns. Regularly posting to your Facebook company page will help your Google search results.

Social media posts are "free campaigns". On LinkedIn, Facebook and Twitter, your company or entity followers will see your posts. When they "like" it (or whatever the jargon on the social media platform), their followers see it. This is how you spread the word – especially on LinkedIn.

LinkedIn is the most serious social media network. It's about quality and not quantity. If you have respected influencers following your page, post content that interests them and get attention from their followers.

Personalized Content Tools

Some of the most amazing marketing tools are the personalized content tools. Every year, they come up with more killer features. Here is what a good personalized content tool does:

- Analyses your website content
- Profiles your visitors demographics and visiting patterns
- Personalizes the content based on a recommended path
- Identifies new and returning users, existing leads, by Google UTM, geography and much more

It's scary when you realize what is going on out there when we visit business websites! No one is forcing anyone to do anything – you are identifying website visitors and displaying your best content to them.

Imagine if a store could do this. You would enter the store, and they would know if you are a new or regular customer. The first aisles you see would be products (clothes, for example) that they know you are interested in. If what you are looking to buy is nearby and not in the back of the store, you are more likely to find it. By having a smooth customer experience, you are more likely to recommend the store to friends.

Real world stores are experts in placing products in the right place. They may not be able to virtually move things like you can on a website (by changing homepage content or top menu items), but the items that are next to the cash register are there for a reason – they sell!

Target Your Influencers

In the past, I would recommend that startups create an Excel spreadsheet of their influencers. There are people out there who want to see your amazing technology in action – find them and let them test drive it. After putting together a list of relevant influencers, someone in the company would contact them directly.

Today, there are too many influencers out there to do it yourself. Everything is fluid and changing quickly over time. Like the personalized content industry within marketing, the influencer industry is fascinating and is growing at the speed of light.

Let's play out a scenario. Your fashion tech/travel tech/cloud/ mobile startup has launched and you have just released your first product. Your website is only starting to receive traction, and initial paid and social media campaigns are taking off.

You know of a few important influencers in your field, but you haven't (and won't) have the time to manually research the top 100 influencers who can help you.

Enter the influencer tool.

Run a search based on keywords and find who are the most influential people who can help your startup. Export a list to Excel, email them, call them, connect with them on LinkedIn, offer them a live demo or free version of your product in order to "wow" them. These people are at the top of the pyramid. One tweet, one like, one share can boost your marketing efforts.

Exit Popups

Imagine being able to know when website visitors are about to leave your site and offer them a popup that encourages them to stay. I've seen the NY Post use this – the website knows when I'm at the bottom of an article, and likely to leave the site. So a popup comes up that hopefully will entice me to click and read more content.

For startups, an exit popup can offer tips, a video or even a plug for you latest product. "Don't leave before you check out ..."

Email Marketing

Email marketing tools were early to appear – by the mid 1990's there were downloadable email marketing tools. Fast forward to today, and many of us are afraid to click on email links and are tired of reading marketing emails.

Still, email marketing works. Today's email marketing tools are obviously SaaS based. Cost is minimal – less than $100 per month will cover your initial needs. The best practice when it comes to email marketing is to email leads. Focus on nurturing existing leads and not on creating new leads out of the blue.

I've seen some CEO's and COO's go overboard when it comes to email marketing. One CEO once showed me his collection of thousands of forms filled out by people who visited the company's booth at conferences over the past 5 years. "Do you realize what I have here", he said, pointing to the paper forms.

"You have nothing," I thought to myself. People who visited your booth 5 years ago aren't leads. Likewise, an email list compiled from nearly a decade ago – or even just a few years ago – aren't leads. Zero relevance. You can spend hours emailing your old email lists, but don't expect much. Spend your time nurturing new leads.

Think of email marketing as a monthly exercise. Spend an hour or so every month emailing new and current leads. If your emails generate business, scale it up.

Surveys

Surveys are a great way to hear the voice of your customers and discover what they like and don't like about your product. Survey tools let you email customers or even put the survey live on your website. You can entice them with Amazon gift cards or with something that your startup can offer.

The more established startups will want to find their "super customers" – like super fans – the paying customers who are thrilled with your product. Not only do you want their feedback, you may want to let them test drive or beta test your upcoming products and upgrades. Their comments can often help R&D and Product to make improvements and deliver a better product.

Surveys is one area where Marketing can help Product. Start a dialogue with your product team and conduct a survey – the effort is minimal compared to the potential value of a quality survey for your startup.

Social Media Monitoring Tools

Keep track of every time your startup, product or technology is mentioned in social media. If you are in a narrow niche, social media monitoring tools can make a huge difference. The sooner you identify who is talking about you, the better.

You can monitor any topic and track your competitors as well.

Live Chat

Speak to them when they're hot! This was a holy grail for years. Today, there are many live chat tools that let you engage with website visitors in real time. There are two scenarios for live chat:

- A website visitor is interested and initiates a live chat session with a click.
- You create a trigger based on number of pages visited, a specific page visited, time on site or even returning visitor and you initiate a live chat session with a website visitor.

By now, most of us are have seen the live chat popups appear within websites that we've visited. When it works, it works wonders. In B2B, I've heard many success stories. This is at least partially due to the high quality of people who are visiting technology B2B websites.

Consider adding Live Chat to your startup. Start off by checking out relevant examples of live chat within your industry.

Product Review Tools

There are many websites out there that offer product reviews. You've likely visited them. Some have built up quite a following and are respected for having quality and in depth reviews of complex technologies.

At one company, I ran a campaign to increase the number of reviews of our software on a few top rated review sites. I sent a survey out to existing customers – three times actually, sent weekly to make sure I captured a good sample. I got a small % of replies.

The next month, I reran the campaign, offering an Amazon gift card. Conversions went through the roof. Finally, I ran the campaign with a crazy high Amazon gift card offer and closed the deal.

Everyone in the company was interested in reading the survey results – the good and bad of what customers had to say.

I isolated the good surveys and ran a campaign to encourage them to post their results on a review site. A bunch did and it made a big difference. But this manual process involved a lot of work and took up most of my time for two months.

Product Review Tools automate this process. They also allow you to collect your best reviews and turn them into content that appear on Google and other websites. There are always new ways to leverage customer reviews – for ecommerce and B2B. See what customer review tools can do for your startup.

eCommerce Tools

eCommerce tools are very advanced. If you are a marketing professional at an ecommerce startup, you will be working with a number of specialized tools. Here is what the other principals in a startup need to know about ecommerce tools:

Some ecommerce tools are end-to-end. They allow you to customize your store, manage inventory, fulfill orders, track sales and customize the user experience – for starters. In this case, you are outsourcing your technology needs to other startups with high expertise in ecommerce. It makes sense unless you have huge inhouse capabilities.

The other major set of ecommerce tools optimize and customize the user experience – at a granular level. When you visit eBay and Amazon, they know exactly what products and content to show you. You can't do this manually. If you are an ecommerce startup, expect to experiment with a few ecommerce tools. Find what works best and scale up.

AB Testing Tools

You have a Get A Demo button on your homepage. How well is it performing? Would it work better with a red background? How will a different message affect conversions? AB testing tools let you create multiple versions of website content and test them.

AB testing is especially important for your homepage – usually your most viewed page. Every pixel and every word can make a difference. When you hit the 50 page mark on your startup website, it may be time to begin a process of AB testing your content. At the minimum, AB test your campaigns and where they lead to, which brings us to the next type of marketing tool.

Landing Page Creation and Testing Tools

Marketing professionals will create dozens, if not hundreds, of landing pages at a startup. Every campaign, every segmentation, every aspect of your landing page and the results should be AB tested. You can do it yourself, or use a landing page tool and gain actionable insights.

A good landing page tool will enable you to test different ideas and implement changes. This is a process that is ongoing. When you start to spend serious money on campaigns, use landing page tools to increase conversions.

It's All About Personalization and Optimization

There are tons of other marketing tools out there that personalize and optimize parts or all of your marketing activities. The more you grow, the more you will rely on these complex marketing tools. My advice is to take it one at a time. You can't afford to spend all of your time implementing and testing new tools. It sure is fun to do! In most cases, you have a small sliver of time allocated to adding new tools. Use it wisely.

Consider what tools are most important and in what priority. You may want Google Analytics and a CRM before you start with AB testing tools. If you're only doing a few social media posts per month, you don't need to spend hours implementing a social media posting tool. Do it yourself until it becomes more practical to automate.

Choosing the right marketing tools is a game of juggling. Read about what's out there. Ask your colleagues at other startups what they use, and try some on your own. The trick is to find the essential tools that help grow your startup.

CHAPTER 8

Meet the Marketing Vendors

When you are a marketing professional at a startup, you will eventually require the services of marketing vendors. The smaller the startup, the sooner you will need them. Marketing vendors offer dozens of marketing services to startups and technology companies. The services offered include:

- Content writing and editing
- Campaign management
- CRM installation and management
- Graphics design
- Marketing automation
- Social media
- Lead generation
- Conferences

In many cases, you are a 1-3 person marketing team. You don't have the luxury of the resources of a large corporation's marketing team that can do most of the work in-house and has agencies to handle the rest. You have to choose what you will do and what you will outsource.

If you are a small startup, perhaps one person on the marketing team and another product professional can handle the content at first. Maybe your need for paid campaigns is basic at first and you can handle them yourself. If you are using a simple CRM, you can have it installed and then run it yourself. Eventually if and when it is time to scale up, you can pass activities to a marketing vendor.

Content Writing & Editing

There are many excellent content writers and writing companies that you can hire to write content for you. They will charge you per article/ word. Make sure your writers are familiar with your technology. Phone calls and even in-person meetings are a good way to give them a quick workshop on what it is you do, and what you believe your message to the world should be. Your outside writers don't spend their days at your startup – the more quality information and feedback you give them, the better the content that you pay for will be.

Ask for writing samples and names of previous and current clients. When you close a deal with a writer or writing service, map out your goals. In the best case scenario, you "place an order" for a steady stream of content – product and technology pages, blog posts, press releases, case studies, thought leadership articles and whatever else you need.

At the end of the day, you – the marketing professional – are responsible for the writing that your writers provide you. Be prepared to edit it yourself or have someone on your team do the editing.

Campaign Management

I always recommend that the startup marketing team lay the foundation for paid campaigns. You need to find the sweet spot of targeting and messaging in order to deliver quality leads. That process should take place from within the startup. Once you find your sweet spot and know what works on various channels, you can outsource it – to save time, or to scale up.

Get your hands dirty on LinkedIn, Facebook, Google AdWords and other paid advertising channels. The more you know about these channels, the better your conversation with your campaign management vendors.

Once you settle on a vendor, put your goals in writing and make sure the vendor believes they can achieve these goals. Like everything else you do, the results of paid campaigns are your results and not just the vendor's. Be an active client. Check and analyze results and suggest ways to increase conversions. It's a numbers game and your goal is to bring in a high number of quality leads.

When it comes to budget, start off low and scale up once you learn what works best. Make sure your quality leads are turning into sales and listen to input from your sales team.

CRM Installation and Management

Raise your hand if you know how to install a CRM.

Not many hands went up. Marketing professionals aren't expected to know how to install and implement a CRM. That's what CRM vendors are for. For the simple CRM's, you may get away with having your web developers run the implementation. If not, expect to pay a CRM vendor.

Before you make any phone calls, map out your funnel. What are you connecting between your website and CRM? What information do you want to flow from one to the other? Is it a "Get A Demo" form or a Contact Us form, both or something else entirely?

Who else will be using your CRM? You want to involve your CEO, VP Sales and sales team and everyone else who will be using the CRM. Get their input on their needs, dashboards and whatever other unique needs your startup has with regards to a CRM.

Now you can reach out to a CRM vendor – a consultant or company – and get a quote. Before you get started, you want to know how much maintenance your CRM will require. For a small startup, the answer may be zero. If you are using Salesforce or another complex CRM, expect to pay a monthly or quarterly fee for CRM maintenance.

In the best case scenario, your CRM runs itself and you focus on generating leads.

Graphics Design

Expect to be working with an outside graphics designer. The start-ups that have in-house designers are often later stage companies that have over 100 employees. The first thing you will be doing with your designer is creating a brand – the logo, website theme and elements and most important – how to visualize your disruptive product.

Face to face meetings and demonstrations can help to communicate to a designer what it is you do and how to go about illustrating your product and its benefits quickly to a wide audience. Often, you need both technology professionals and the business to understand what it is you do.

Once your website is live, you will always be creating new content – new content which requires design. For blog posts, you can save time and resources by using a stock photo service and cropping the photos yourself. Buy a subscription that fits your needs and consider sharing it with your designer. You'll both be using it. Consult with your designer before going with a stock photo service – which service is currently considered the best and perhaps your designer can get you a discount.

Beyond the website and blog posts, you and your designer will be responsible for all aspects of conferences – the physical booth and printed brochures. Other common pieces of content which require design include case studies, press releases and datasheets. Create templates for each so you can whip up new assets quickly, and when you change designers, you will be able to onboard them as easily as possible.

Match your content to design. What content are you creating, and what will do you yourself and what requires a designer?

Marketing Automation

If you are a later stage startup and/or have a complex funnel, you may find yourself working with one or more complicated marketing automation tools. If this is the case and you don't have a team member who is a marketing automation expert, you will need to find a marketing automation vendor.

A good marketing automation vendor can do magic with a well-designed and flowing funnel. If you have a greased and oiled lead generation machine, smart marketing automation can scale things up and massively increase conversions. Basically, marketing automation ensures that no lead falls through the cracks, and leads receive the right information for their segment and stage in the funnel. You can do this manually with a small number of new leads per month, but with hundreds or more, marketing automation is the only way to properly move leads through the funnel.

Marketing automation vendors will be familiar and experienced with all of the latest tools. The tools themselves may change over time, but expect them to get more powerful and more complex to run. Before you meet with a marketing automation professional, consider these points:

Do you know your funnel inside and out? If you don't know your funnel, how will an outside expert? Create a document with a summary and illustration of your current lead flow.

What are the strong and weak points of your funnel? Where do things slow down – at the beginning or at the end?

Speak to your sales team and ask them if there is anything they need when it comes to marketing automation. Are they notified when new leads enter the system? Are the right people updated when leads do something on your website? Are leads receiving the right content?

What are your marketing needs for a marketing automation system? Consider email marketing, customized content and read up on the latest new features in marketing automation. Every few months – or even more often – there are new killer features that you may want to implement on your side.

When you meet with a consultant, communicate the above and ask what else you could add that you didn't think of. You will likely discover more options to consider.

When you build your startup's marketing automation, consider the resources required to maintain it and make sure that your tools serve you and not the other way around. Don't scale up too early or too late.

Social Media

At first, you should be able to handle social media on your own. Every time you create a piece of content, you want to distribute it – usually via social media. I call these "free campaigns". If you only have a few posts a week or less, you don't need a social media vendor.

When you ramp up your content marketing, consider hiring a social media vendor. Social media evolves and changes quickly. The character counts, formatting and distribution options change over time. A social media professional will know all this and more. A big part of social media marketing is knowing when and how often to post content. When your marketing machine grows, you want to maximize incoming leads from your social media followers; they are at the entry point of your funnel.

Lead Generation

There are many marketing vendors who offer various lead generation services. This is different than managing campaigns. They typically hawk lead lists or offer to "bring in x leads" in a short amount of time.

First, make sure what they are offering is legal where you are located and where you are targeting your marketing efforts. It's hit or miss – you can spend hundreds to thousands of dollars and get excellent new leads, or nothing.

Lead generation efforts are similar to the percentage of risk you take in a stock portfolio. Investors sometimes take 1-5% of their stock portfolio and invest in riskier companies. If they fall, they lose a small, controlled number. If one of the companies succeeds, even once in a while, it justifies the risk.

If you are impressed with a lead generation vendor's reputation and services, consider how much it will cost and what it would take for your startup to benefit from the leads.

Even where it is 100% legal, I am not a big fan of buying leads. Leads need to be nurtured. Old lead lists from years ago are worthless today. Your best leads are the ones who gravitate to your startup on their own.

A lead generation vendor may offer a smart way for your startup to benefit from LinkedIn and better target prospects. Look into tools that you can manage yourself and speak to colleagues about their successes and failures with lead generation vendors.

Conferences

Preparing a startup for a conference is a fulltime job – for one or more people. There are tons of logistics to handle and on top of that you have marketing and sales goals. If your attendance at a conference does not include a booth, you create assets (brochures, business cards) with your designer and prepare the sales team with whatever else they need.

If your startup will be hosting a booth, prepare to be busy for at least 3 months. This is where a conference vendor comes in. The conference vendor knows all of the logistics of the major technology conferences. This is especially good for a small startup that is planning a booth. A small startup may not have a marketing team – it may be only you.

Many conference vendors offer marketing services. They have a game that booth visitors play that isolates quality leads, or some mechanism to attract the right people to your booth. If you are already spending $50k or more to host a booth, consider the potential ROI on spending another $10k and coming home with a terrific hot leads list.

Like the other parts of this chapter, map out your logistics, marketing and sales needs before you reach out to a conference vendor. Conferences bring marketing and sales together – prepare your conference with your sales team and learn from their experience.

Expect the unexpected. There are so many things that can go wrong heading into a conference. An important item doesn't arrive, weak internet connection, someone doesn't show up. Decide ahead of time what you or others will do when every likely bad scenario happens. Who will run to the store? If the internet is weak, can you run whatever it is you are running on local computers or a makeshift network? What is the involvement of your conference vendor during the show – whether they attend or work off-site?

CHAPTER 9

Content

C ontent is the fuel of startup marketing. Content fuels your website, brand, PR efforts, marketing tools and campaigns. Before you learn to excel at the other aspects of startup marketing, become an expert in content marketing. In this section, I will explore content from a startup marketing perspective. I strongly encourage startup marketing professionals to become writers and not just editors.

The Headline

Content begins with a headline. Despite its short length, the headline is the most important part of any piece of content. Decades ago, advertising pioneer David Ogilvy wrote, "On average, five times as many people read the headline as read the body copy. When you have written your headline, you have spent eighty cents of your dollar."

That is true today. We are bombarded with headlines and only click or read what really interests us.

Feature, Benefit and Dream

Let's take a look at an imaginary soundbar. It has a new "Crazy Sound" component inside which enables the soundbar to sound much better than anything else on the market.

"Crazy Sound" is the feature

Incredible sound quality is the benefit

"The best sound system you ever imagined you could afford" is the dream

The topic of feature, benefit and dream comes up often at startups. Many startup sites focus on the features and you can spend an hour reading about heavy technology features without grasping the benefits. Startups typically know how to express the dream; the challenge is drilling down to the benefits.

The features speak to the technology professionals. The benefits speak to the business. The dream speaks to investors. Weave all three together in every piece of content.

Before you sit down to write or "place an order" for content to your writer, consider where the focus should be. A product page should have both features and benefits with a touch of the dream. An investment press release should focus on the dream. A case study may focus on the features or benefits, depending on the audience. Blog posts should cover features, benefits and the dream.

---

7 Types of Headlines

There are many ways to categorize headlines. These seven reflect startups and technology. The next time you need to write a headline, consider which of these seven make the most sense based on your message and audience. Try writing a few types of headlines and A/B test them – whether by asking your colleagues for feedback or running a real A/B test online.

Discount – "Save up to 30%.."

New Feature/Benefit/Dream – "The new xyz will enable your business to .." "Imagine being able to ..."

Question – "Do you want to .." "Have you ever tried"

Testimonial – "Xyz saved us a lot of time and money"

How To – "5 tips on ..." "10 ways to ..." "3 reasons you should ..."

Guarantee – "Do xyz and you are guaranteed to ..."
Tired Of – "Are you tired of ..." "Are you suffering from ..." "Is xyz slowing you down?"

Write and edit hundreds of headlines. Even if you have a content writer, you will gain insight on the headline writing process. The faster your startup grows, the less time you will have for writing. On a few occasions, I found myself sitting with the CEO trying to come up with a short headline that explains a disruptive technology. This headline would become the company's catch phase or slogan. The more complex the technology, the harder it is to come up with a headline.

Look around you and pay more attention to the headlines of the day. What words or phrases trigger you to click on a news headline? What headlines trigger you to click or read more when you visit technology websites? Take a look at other startups in your field and see what they do. You may or may not like what you see.

Blog Posts

Once you've mastered the art of headlines, move onto blog posts. The startup blog should be fun to read. Whatever it is your startup does, there is some sort of heavy technology. Lighten it up a bit. Blogs are not collections of datasheets. The startup blog should reflect the culture of the startup.

The startup blog is often the first area of your site that people will encounter. Over time, there will be a lot more blog posts than any other type of content and the blog will be well indexed in Google. Your blog is a gateway. It needs to please all audiences – technology, business and investors. When I visit a website and see a barely used blog, I take note. Some startups have very active blogs which are a lot more interesting to read than datasheets and product pages.

Ask other people in your startup if they want to participate in the blog. If someone says yes, meet with that person for an hour. Come up with an interesting topic to write about based on that person's role in the company. For your VP Product, you can write about a new killer feature. For your VP Sales, you can write about an experience at a conference or with a happy customer. For your CEO, you can write about "the dream".

You or someone on your marketing team "ghost writes" the article and it is posted in the interviewee's name. It adds a touch of life to your blog when posts are from a variety of real people. Even if you only do this a few times a year, it is worth the effort. I've enjoyed ghost writing blog posts with my colleagues who work in product, customer success, sales and R&D. It's a good way to connect with others and learn from them. They end up with a blog post in their name that they edited and approved.

In general, blog posts should be 300 to 1,000 words and of course you can go as long as you want. Google changes the rules every so often – read up on the latest word count recommendations.

Every new piece of top level content that you create can also be a blog post.

Turn your startup's blog into a printing press and release a lot of content! Every new piece of top level content that you post or release justifies and should trigger a blog post. When you run a press release, write a condensed version on your blog with a link to the press release. When you release a new product or product version, write about it on your blog with a link to more content. When your startup attends a conference, write about it. For every new piece of content, ask yourself, "Can we rewrite this and get a blog post out of it?"

If your startup attends a conference, you have another good source of blog post content. Months before the conference, let the world know that you will be attending. In the month preceding the conference, write weekly or bi-weekly posts on what your team will be demonstrating or doing at the conference. Try to get a few people who are attending the conference to work with you on ghost written blog posts. If you are lucky, someone will agree to send you daily updates while they are at the conference and you can post short daily updates on your blog for a sense of "live action". Finally, when the conference is over, post a summary of your startup's activities and achievements at the conference.

When your product team is preparing a new major release, meet with your VP Product and discuss a product marketing rollout plan. This may include datasheets, product pages and blog posts. The blog posts are "teasers" of the long form content that you create. One detailed product page can be turned into a few blog posts – every major feature/benefit can be discussed with testimonials and content with a lighter tone on the blog.

Speaking of case studies, turn every case study into a blog post. You can end it with a teaser and encourage readers to read the entire case study. "Company xyz faced challenges. What did they do when they ..."

If you are at a B2B startup with a complex technology, there is no getting around adding heavy technical content to your blog. Yes, the blog should show a lighter side of things. When you are selling a complex product, it takes complex words to convey your message and the blog is a great place to "continue on where the product and technology pages left off."

Take a look at your product and technology pages. If you have good material to work with, you will find dozens of scenarios and use cases to write about. Connect with someone on your product or R&D team. The heavy content requires a technical partner. The VP Product is the best person to start with. Agree on a blog post schedule – 1 or 2 a month is fine as this is a long term project. At first, you will need their time and even writing. As you learn more about your startup's product and technology, you may be able to handle more of the content. An outside content writer or a content writer without an extensive technology background will not be able to write technical blog posts – on their own or with product team members.

I've found that these highly technical blog posts, that cover specific use cases and scenarios are often the most read and shared pages on a startup's website. This is what your target audience is Googling and researching.

Finally, zoom out and write thought leadership articles. Go beyond your startup's features and write about the dreams of your industry. Educate technology decision makers with your vision. I've worked with startup CEO's and CTO's on thought leadership articles that were posted on the blog and on external news sites. In one hour, you can learn more deep information about your startup than you did in the previous three months. It can take more than one session to flesh out the story and ideas. Expect to write 1,500 to 3,000 words for thought leadership blog posts as well as an extended editing process.

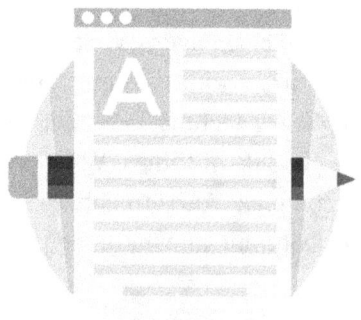

The Product/Technology Pages and Datasheet

The product and technology pages as well as the datasheet (a one pager that covers both product and technology) are the first pieces of content that marketing will tackle at a startup. If your startup doesn't have a website, you begin with the core content. The product and technology pages aren't "just" pieces of top level content. They *are* your startup!

What do you want industry analysts to know? What do you want your decision makers and influencers to know? What content should be featured on top? What mix of business and technology content do you want? What features, benefits and dream do you need to depict?

The owner of the product and technology pages is the VP Product. Marketing's role is to help the product team to turn their features, benefits and dream into quality content. Work closely with a partner on the product team or the company founders – whatever the case. Expect to have many sessions discussing the concepts and come up with a "new language" to communicate your disruptive technology and product.

The pages themselves should be a mix of words, bulleted phrases and photos and illustrations. Product pages are not essays. Read other product and technology pages and determine what styles and mix of content formats you like. The style and design are very important. Bring in your graphics designer and have them give you a few templates and options.

If you find your pages to be too long, play the role of editor and remove the pieces of "TMI" – too much information. You can always add additional pages that answer detailed questions or zoom in on a specific point that the general audience may not be interested in.

When you have finished versions of your product and technology pages, turn them into one or two datasheets. If it is possible, one datasheet can portray both your product and technology on one concise page. If not, create two – one for each. Datasheets are handouts to give people at conferences and meetings. Later on, you can create multi-page brochures. It is a good exercise for product and marketing to be forced into a room to decide how to "say it all" on one page, verbally and visually. Create PDF and Word versions of your datasheets and pass them onto sales and everyone else who needs them.

Finally, your product and technology pages are a source for future content. Press releases, blog posts, campaigns and case studies will all borrow content from your core product and technology content.

The Homepage

The homepage is similar to the headline in that it is all-important. Once you have your product and technology pages, you can begin to consider what will appear on the homepage.

The homepage weaves your product and technology into a story that flows from top to bottom. On the top is a bold message that your decision makers and influencers should instantly connect with. As you scroll down, each section tells your startup's story. A common startup homepage flow is:

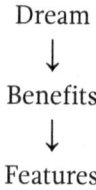

Dream
↓
Benefits
↓
Features

The top section of a startup's homepage should "wow" you. B2B or B2C, you had better impress your audience within 5 seconds with a dream.

The next section of the startup homepage should cover the benefits – "What's in it for me?" What are the 3-5 most amazing benefits to using your product? Stick with the big picture and stay away from obscure benefits that will leave the other 90% of your audience scratching their heads. Speak with your product and sales colleagues to come up with a list of the top 3 benefits in the order you choose.

Next you discuss the features. In some cases, features and benefits are so intertwined, that they are hard to separate. If this is the case, cover them on one section of the homepage. The features section can drill down and get more technical.

Finally you have the bottom content of the page where you summarize everything and offer a call to action (which should also be available on the top of the page). Testimonials are a good way to "make closing arguments" to decision makers.

If your startup is very active, consider adding a section to your homepage with dynamic content – articles, news, conference photos and whatever else you can come up with. Add new dynamic content every week or few weeks so your homepage doesn't appear to be "too static" year after year.

Press Releases

Press releases pre-date the internet by decades. Things haven't changed much as far as style and goals. A new product, product feature, major business deal or partnership are triggers for press releases. PR Newswire and Business Wire are the two major players. Read up on press releases from other companies in your field and in general.

The headline is by far the most important part of a press release. Yes, 10 words are worth infinitely more than the next 600 words. You are competing against hundreds or thousands of new press releases released daily. If you want to get attention and build a brand, invest a lot of time into your press release headline. How can you express your dream into a concise headline? What are the 3 or so words that have to appear in the headline? Now find the right verbs to connect them and add an adjective or two.

The first paragraph is the second most important part of a press release. Here, you restate the headline and add a few powerful sentences. Think about your startup's dream – use the strongest words possible to communicate your message. The headline filters who will read your first paragraph. The first paragraph filters who will read the rest of your press release.

The next few paragraphs should feature quotes from your CEO, founders or whoever is relevant drilling down and commenting on the "big message". If the first paragraph is about the dream, then these paragraphs are about the benefits and features.

Finally, the last paragraph or two are about your startup. This is called a "boilerplate" – 3-6 sentences about your startup and product which serves as the bottom content on press releases and other documents.

If you are distributing your press release via PR Newswire or Business Wire, consider paying extra to add an illustration or photo. In the past, I've used illustrations from the product and technologies pages that "say it all" visually. If a picture is worth a thousand words, a press release picture may cost a thousand dollars or more. But it is worth it.

Case Studies

Case studies are incredibly important pieces of content in B2B startups. Your blog and homepage are the entry points to your funnel. Product and technology pages and similar "deep content" are in the middle of your funnel. Case studies are at the end of your funnel. By the time prospects read your case studies, they know all about your features, benefits and dream.

At this stage, they want to read about real experiences of real people discussing the challenges that lead to their using your product and of course how your product dealt with those challenges.

Case studies often originate from the customer success, product and sales teams. Someone has to get a customer to agree to do a case study. Often a sales professional will have good relations with a certain customer who likes your company and product. Sometimes the VP Product works with a few customers on new features and these customers are great for offering deep insight on your product's value and ROI. A case study can land from anywhere. When it does, marketing should schedule a one hour conversation with the contact on the other side.

Prepare for your first few case study calls ahead of time. Think of the end result and the sections within a case study. They are:

- About the company
- Challenges faced
- Solution
- Results

Prepare questions accordingly:

Tell me about your company and your role. What do you and your
team do?

What challenges did you face and what brought you to look at our
company? Did you also try other solutions?

Describe the solution that my company offered you and why your
side agreed to use it.

What are/were the results? Can you give me numbers and an ROI
statement?

What would you like to tell other companies facing the same
challenges?

What would you say to those who are skeptical regarding this
solution?

How was the onboarding experience and how is customer success/
support?

Add any specific questions based on your startup's product and give
them a call. Take good notes and head straight for the keyboard after
the conversation ends and type it all up.

Now you need a case study template. A case study template is based
on the headers – company, challenges, solution, results. You can create a text version of the template and have a designer create a standard
template for use on the web and PDF.

Create a new text document, and use your phone call notes to create the content you need that fits exactly into each section of your case
study template. Figure out what the rough word count is for each section. Add a few text boxes with the best quotes/testimonials.

When you write the case study headline, use the ROI statement and/or the most powerful quote that fits your needs.

The next step is critical – get the case study approved by both sides. In most cases, the customer will approve the case study with few or no changes. It was written to make both sides look good in the first place and there is no controversial content in a case study. Sometimes, the other side will stonewall approval. There's not much you can do about it when a c-level at another company won't sign off on a piece of content.

Try to generate a continual pipeline of case studies. Even adding one case study per quarter and ending up with four every year is a lot better than one or none.

Now that you have approval, not only do you have a case study, you can write a blog post and share the case study on social media. The link can be either to the case study web page or to your blog. The blog version can be either a rewrite of the case study or a short teaser version covers the challenges and ends with, "Click here to read how xyz company overcame this challenge!"

Webinars

A webinar is a serious piece of spoken content. Webinars are similar to case studies in that they are helpful in closing a deal with prospects. Anyone who spends a half hour watching a presentation about your product or topic is a potentially good lead. In most cases, that person has already read a lot of other content on your website and is looking for a deeper discussion on your product, technology or dream.

Typically, a webinar is based on a PowerPoint presentation. Marketing will definitely need a strong partner from product or R&D in order to produce a webinar. The product/R&D partner is the source of thought leadership, not marketing. The two should sides should discuss a number of potential webinar topics.

Next, pick one of the topics and run with it. Meet with whoever you are working with and create a PowerPoint presentation that tells the story you want to tell. Use short phrases and bulleted content on the presentation. You can write your "screenplay" – the spoken part – in notes on each slide that the viewer won't see.

Send your text presentation to your graphics designer. You can create a webinar PowerPoint template so you can do the design yourself after the first time, and just add stock photos and illustrations as needed.

Do a practice run. How long is your presentation? Is your presentation focused? Now, record your webinar. Determine whether your webinar will be gated content or not. In most cases, you want to ask viewers to fill out a form so you know who they are. Some startups run live webinars, but those are major productions for a small startup with a 1-3 person marketing team. Record it and have your web developers do their thing so the webinar is featured on your website with a lead form.

Finally, decide what to do with webinar leads with your sales team. Sales professionals may ask you to email webinar participants and they may decide to call each one of them. Track results. Do webinars help to close deals?

eBooks

eBooks are a great way to move leads through your funnel with long form content. Like webinars, eBooks should be gated behind a form. Consider the stages of your funnel when you are looking for eBook topics.

Let's use a soundbar for example.

Stage 1 eBooks could be "5 tips to improving your existing sound system", or "How to ..."

Stage 2 eBooks could be "How to resolve the most common technical issues when connecting devices to your soundbar".

Stage 3 eBooks could be "How to choose a new soundbar" or "5 features every new soundbar should have".

The people who read the stage 1 eBooks are interested in sound systems. Those who read the stage 2 eBooks are more experienced with sound systems and are looking to resolve challenges. Finally, the stage 3 eBook audience is getting ready to choose a new solution.

Map out your startup's 3 stages if you haven't already. Make a list of eBook topics for each stage. Start with stage 1 – you need a lot of funnel opener content – and move your way up. An eBook should be a few thousand words. Add design and even a template if you plan on producing many eBooks. Make sure you have your company info on the back, and of course, a call to action even on a PDF.

If you have a good email list of prospects, decide which group gets which eBooks based on who they are and their stage in your funnel. Produce eBooks at a realistic pace – start at one per quarter and end a year with four quality eBooks.

Go over your existing content and see if you can transform any of it to an eBook. A thought leadership piece, a strong blog post, a webinar or a case study can be "recycled" into an eBook.

Landing Pages

As soon as you start running campaigns, you will need to create landing pages. Even if you use a landing page or marketing automation tool, it is up to you to decide what will be displayed on your landing pages.

Landing page content and design are very important. Anyone who is on a landing page already took an action and clicked on something in order to arrive on the landing page. You have a chance at grabbing their attention. Make the most of it.

Start with landing page design. Find or create a pleasant and easy to use template. Simplicity is the key word – landing pages should not be "busy". They should be easy to read and everything should flow to the call to action.

The text of a typical landing page should be as follows:

Headline
2-3 sentences
3-5 bullets
Closing sentence
Call to action

You don't have the luxury of multiple paragraphs. Your audience expects a brief message that gets right to the point.

Start with the end – the call to action. What is your call to action? It can be get a demo, contact us, try it now, request more info or whatever it is that you are pushing. On the technical side, the call to action button or text should connect to your CRM and marketing automation tools.

Once you know the end of the story, you head to the beginning – the all-mighty headline. Create a headline that is direct, powerful and clear. Next, write a few sentences that expand on your topic. Add a few bullets based on the features, benefit or dream. A bulleted list is a good design element for landing pages – a lot easier to read than a second paragraph.

Finally, a closer. One or two sentences that summarize the offering. Below it, the call to action.

There are many tools that enable you to A/B test your landing pages. Figure out what works best as far as types of headlines, text and design.

Blog as a Landing Page

Landing pages are typically created as an "island". There is only one link on the page – the call to action. That's both good and bad. Your website audience knows what a landing page is. They recognize that there are no other links on the page. They may not be ready to fill out a form. Maybe you didn't make your case to them yet or they are hesitant to give you their email address and info.

I have found that "blog as a landing page" is the perfect alternative to the island style landing page. With blog as a landing page, you send leads from a campaign (paid or free) to the blog. Add a form to the end of every blog post. Not a link to a form, but the form itself. Add this same "form on a page" to many other pages – as many as you are comfortable with. This allows your audience to learn more about your offering and fill out a form when they are ready. In a way, blog as a landing page gives more options to the audience and shows them a bit of respect by telling them, "Go ahead, read more about our amazing product and let us know when you want to try it out!"

Those who are immediately ready will fill out the form. With an island landing page, you just lost the other 99%. With blog as a landing page, you are giving the other 99% a second and third chance to fill out the form.

Emails

Email marketing is still alive and kicking. Everyone likes to put it down, but if you have a quality list of leads, you can use email marketing to move them along the funnel. Success numbers will be low, but people do click on good emails and you need every win you can get.

Every time someone fills out a form, you get their name, email address, company and title. After conferences, you should get hundreds of new email addresses. Every piece of gated content – webinars and eBooks – provides email addresses. You also have the email addresses of existing customers.

The first type of email you can send out is the "discount offer". Offer a 20% discount on new purchases and/or renewals or whatever applies to your business model. For startups selling products that cost well into the 5 digit numbers, your CEO and VP Sales may not agree to run discount offer emails. This is fair and it is their call to make. High end companies have every right to decide not to offer mass discounts to a large audience. They typically discount the final purchase order, but don't want to announce their discounts to the world.

The next type of email is the "conference email". A month before your startup attends a conference, you will likely add a page or pages to your website. Send a series of emails that follow your conference messaging and goals. Coordinate ahead of time with your sales team.

We move onto the "product launch" email. A few times a year you are launching a new product or major version release. Email blast it.

Onto the "content email". You are constantly producing and assembling more quality content – eBooks, webinars, datasheets, case studies and blog posts. A good way to keep in touch with leads is to send them a monthly email to your best new content. It will help push them further into your funnel.

The "news email" lets everyone know about a notable event or media coverage regarding your startup. When you make it to a major news site, you may want to let everyone know.

When it comes to writing style, emails are similar to landing pages. The headline is the subject. The body of the email is the rest – the sentences, bullets, closing sentence and call to action. Keep emails short and to the point. No one will read more than a few sections of text on an email. Apply the same lessons you learn from other short forms of content to emails – headlines, landing pages and ad content.

A note of caution – don't overdo it and don't overestimate potential results from email marketing. Count every sales qualified lead that comes in via email marketing as a bonus. I've had COO's push me to send more and more emails, thinking that the more we send, the more leads we will have. If email marketing is your lead savior, you have a problem. Focus on other more modern marketing techniques and channels and run email marketing quietly in the background.

Ad Banners and Text Ads

Writing the text for ad banners and text ads is challenging. You are given a tiny word count to convince an audience to click. Getting people to click on ads is getting harder and harder over time. We are a lot more suspicious of clicking than we were decades ago.

In the 1990's and early 2000's, I was able to get click-through rates of 5-20%. I would take the ads that my advertisers sent me and improve them. If I could get a 3% click-through rate up to 15%, the advertiser would be very happy and continue advertising.

Today, a 1% click-through rate is considered excellent and is even a few times higher than you need in order to succeed.

There is only one way to go about writing ad content – powerful words with a clear call to action. Create strong headlines – you have 5-15 words in most cases to make your offer 100% clear. Use command verbs and get to the point. A/B test your best ad copy and learn what works best as far as clicks and generating new sales.

Quarterly Report

At every startup, the VP Marketing will have to create and present a quarterly report. If you go by the calendar year, start working on it on the first day of the new quarter and let your CEO know when it will be ready. Create a template and your following quarterly reports will be easier to assemble.

The quarterly report should cover the entire funnel. The first page should get right to the bottom line, as follows:

Total Spent - $100,000	Leads	Cost Per Lead
Leads That Became Sales	100	$1,000
Sales Qualified Leads	1,000	$100
Marketing Leads	10,000	$10

In the above example table, marketing spent $100,000. The cost per type of lead is clear. In the following pages, you can drill down on website traffic with Google Analytics numbers. How many website visitors do you have per quarter? What countries and pages are performing the best?

Create pages or slides for every major marketing activity – campaigns, conferences, case studies – and make your case.

Many startups have a quarterly business review – QBR – whereby every department creates a quarterly report and presents it to everyone or the senior brass. It is a great experience to produce a quarterly report and defend you and your team's actions and results. I've been at a few very interesting QBR's which led to deeper discussions on other ways to achieve results and how other departments can work with marketing to make it happen.

A Final Word on Content

The only way to become a good writer is to write. Try writing each type of content covered in this book – blog posts, headlines, product pages, datasheets and eBooks. Learn what types of content you are better at and what is more challenging. Read from many sources and as you write, you will develop your own style. Startup writing isn't easy – the content is complex and the audience is very demanding. Every startup has to become good at producing quality content quickly in order to survive.

CHAPTER **10**

Social Media

W hat happens when you mix social media with online tracking tools? The result is scary. For the same reason that I love social media as a marketing professional, I abhor many aspects of it as a private person.

The internet's basic technology is to connect people and things. In the 1990's and 2000's, we connected with people nonstop. In the past few years, we have all been exposed to the dark side of social media – trolls, tracking and criminal activity.

We're no longer in the Garden of Eden. The innocence of social media is a thing of the past. When social media gained traction in the mid-2000's, many of us enjoyed filling out forms and telling Facebook what we liked and what we did. Today, we understand what the social media giants did with that information. Some of that information was used ethically and legally – cookies that track your internet habits. Some of that information was used illegally, by hacks, breaches and blunders.

The more I learned about what I can do with social media at work, the less I wanted to participate in social media at home.

Nonetheless, social media is an important tool for marketing professionals. Your targets are seeking information on social media and you are tasked with milking the cow.

Social Media Planning

Discuss your social media plans with the rest of your marketing team and your CEO. Sales professionals aren't usually interested in your company's Facebook presence – they are more interested in what goes on at the end of the funnel.

Social media is your funnel opener.

Begin with company pages on LinkedIn, Facebook, Twitter, Instagram, YouTube and whatever other social media networks are somewhat relevant to your startup. Work with your graphics designer to get the right photo resolutions for each social network. Create a blurb about your startup and add it to your company page. Add any other content that you have – photos for Facebook, videos for YouTube, etc.

Post It!

Once you have your social media pages setup, start posting content. Every new blog post should be followed by social media posts referring and linking to the content. Post your news, conference campaigns and of course new product launches. Start off with 1-2 social media posts a week and grow your audience.

Growing a social media audience takes time. It is similar to long-term investing. You may see results in a month, but it takes 6 months to a year to organically grow an audience. It takes years of hard work on social media to create a powerful presence with tens of thousands of followers.

Track your social media posts with Google UTMs. You want to know when leads begin their journey on your funnel via social media. What content stirs up the most comments, likes and shares? What content brings in followers and what content generates leads?

Involve Others

Your startup's social media presence is a part of the brand and should reflect your startup's values. Involve others in your social media activities. Write blog posts with members of your startup, giving them the credit for the post. If they aren't writers, sit with them and take notes. Be their ghost writer. When you post the blog post, post/promote it on social media.

It is good for your startup to have multiple people participating in getting your message out. This includes everyone – the CEO, VP Product, VP Sales, VP R&D and even Customer Success.

I've had great experiences writing blog posts with Product and Customer Success colleagues. We agree on a topic and meet for an hour. While discussing the topic, I take notes and later write an article. After a few edits, the article is posted. They get a souvenir to add to their LinkedIn profile and show their friends and the startup gets an important message distributed to thousands of people.

Find the people at your startup who are willing to work with you on this. Blog posts from startup team members are a terrific way to push your message to decision makers. As a bonus, you will have a chance to interact with people who you perhaps don't otherwise interact with at your startup.

Get Everyone Involved Part 2

When you post content on social media, send an email to all of your startup colleagues and ask them to share and like the post. CEO's appreciate this. I don't expect every programmer to be active on social media, but if I catch a few who are, it helps. I do expect product and sales professionals to share and like content. Some people are more active than others.

Draw the line between LinkedIn and the rest. It is one thing to ask someone to like or share LinkedIn content, it is another to ask someone to like or share Facebook content. While I ask everyone to embrace the startup's Facebook page, I don't expect it. LinkedIn is a professional social network. Many people separate their professional and personal lives and they have the right to.

You'll end up with many colleagues who are active on LinkedIn and a few who are active on Facebook.

Hunting For Leads On Social Media

Leave no social media stone unturned. Take a daily or weekly look at your likes and shares. See if any of them are potential decision makers. If so, send an email with information to your sales team. Maybe someone can strike up a conversation with the person and turn a like into a lead.

Tell Your Story

The average follower will see your social media posts for a few seconds at a time a few times a month. Tell your startup's story on your social media pages. Post a mix of technical and product content as well as content geared for the business and a wider audience. Invest time in choosing the right photos for your posts – people are bombarded with content and images. Find a suitable way to stand out from the crowd.

Automate Your Social Media

When your startup grows and you have a larger audience and are post-ing content more frequently, consider using a social media automation tool to automate posts. Instead of manually visiting Facebook, LinkedIn and sometimes many more social media sites, a good tool allows you to paste the content once, make changes based on social media platform character counts and formatting differences.

Next, the social media automation tool can decide the optimal time to post the content and how often. The micro details of social media are always evolving, and a tool lets you leverage the latest best practices without having to learn them yourself.

B2B — Focus on LinkedIn

LinkedIn is a powerful tool for B2B. You can identify, generate and target leads with LinkedIn and much more. I've met sales professionals who are absolute wizards at making the most of LinkedIn. Read up on the latest LinkedIn tools and premium account features. Speak with your sales team and discuss which tools and features can help generate sales qualified leads.

B2C — Focus on Facebook

If you are a consumer facing startup, Facebook will likely be your primary social media marketing tool. Facebook lets you communicate to a huge audience for free. Run both free and paid campaigns on Facebook. They work hand-in-hand to generate leads.

Fine tune your content marketing so your posts go viral. Excite people with engaging content. Photos are much more important on Facebook than on LinkedIn. Things move fast on Facebook, so be ready to automate your Facebook presence early on if Facebook is an important marketing channel.

CHAPTER **11**

Public Relations

Public relations is the odd man out in startup marketing. In many ways, public relations precedes technology startups. PR agencies were essentially doing the same thing in the 1970's for non-tech – creating buzz and building brands. Both B2B and B2C businesses need a smart public relations strategy in order to succeed. The same tactics used today to promote technology startups were developed in the previous century by David Ogilvy and other public relations innovators in the 1960's to 1980's.

How is PR the odd man out? One mantra of startup marketing is "Everything I do is measurable." PR is barely measurable in the short term and only really measurable over a period of years. Building a brand requires a lot of activities that typically take a long time to bear fruit. PR spending can become a spending trap for startups who rely too much on it and too little on lead generation.

Let's look at an example.

A startup spends $10k a month at a PR agency over a period of 3 years. Every week, the marketing team conducts a conference call with the PR agency. Pitches are sent to the media, press releases go out every quarter and key industry journalists are identified and gently pushed towards your new product and technology breakthroughs. PR agencies also help when it comes to analysts, such as Gartner and Forrester.

The results after 3 years? A few articles per year in "high ranked" news sites and journals pertaining to your startup and a few dozen article and mentions among the "rest of the pack" of niche news sites and journals. A few noted journalists visited your conference booths and were treated to one-on-one demos.

Is that worth $100k a year for a total of $300k? It depends on your budget and your needs.

Some startup CEO's that I've worked with don't like PR at all. Many of those CEO's approved a PR budget, but perhaps were more realistic as to the possible immediate results. It makes sense. The CEO of a hardcore SaaS startup isn't expecting to build the next McDonald's or Coca Cola. One CEO who I worked with approved funding for our PR efforts even though he was skeptical. He and his CTO knew how to give flawless presentations to Gartner and that made a huge difference. Looking back, the Gartner and Forrester presentations helped the company more than the sprinkling of media articles about the company.

If your top goal is to get the attention of industry analysts and appear in the media, PR will do wonders at a high cost. With a $100k a year marketing budget, you probably can't afford a full service PR agency. A marketing budget of $1M or more a year is in the right place to consider hiring a PR agency.

Strategies For Improving Your Startup's Public Relations Efforts

Whether you are working with a PR agency or not, you should create a spreadsheet with your target journalists and journals. I'm not referring to the Wall Street Journal and Wired! Those two of course are the cream of the crop when it comes to media. Begin with your niche. If you are a travel tech startup, make a list of the travel tech news sites and prominent writers. Whatever your sector, there are news sites and journals that cover your field. Spend a few hours compiling a list.

If you work with a PR agency, show them your list and ask them if they have anything you missed. If you don't work with a PR agency, consider reaching out to these news sites and journals. When a new product launches, let them know. Send your press release with a personal note. Offer a one-on-one demo. Build relations with relevant media outlets.

When you sign a contract to work with a PR agency, make sure everyone on your team understands what you are signing and what the expectations are. Don't oversell that your startup could be in Time Magazine or the NY Times within a few months! Align expectations with your PR agency. Because of the nature of the business, they are hesitant to commit to measurable goals. That game is changing thanks to exposure to the measurable world of online marketing. If you are going to spend $50k-$100k a year on a PR agency, there is nothing wrong with asking for a list of achievable goals. In the long run, the move is towards a hybrid model – retainer + payment for success.

Message is Everything

No matter how good your PR agency is, everything depends on your killer message. Consider how many press releases go out every day, every week. Another partnership between two companies, another minor feature added to a product, another company is "proud to announce" something that you will forget in five minutes.

Consider how your press release will stand out from the crowd. How can you blow people away with a 10-15 word headline? A lot depends on your technology and product. With a boring product, there's not much buzz you can create. If you are lucky enough to be marketing an exciting product, invest a lot of time in your message. Work with your CEO, VP Product and VP Sales and get it right. The headline and first paragraph are the most important. The rest is essentially filler – the usual quotes and comments. Make the first five sentences matter.

A Final Note on Public Relations

Every few months, compare your PR goals with the results. If after a year into paying $10k a month, you are not getting solid results, speak with others on your team. Is it your messaging? Is it the product? Is the PR agency delivering reasonable, average or poor results? When you are investing thousands of dollars per month on public relations, you have every right to eventually analyze results and expect something tangible. Know when to pause your PR efforts and when to shop around for a new agency. When your marketing budget is cut, you may need to spend less on PR and move more funds to lead generation efforts.

CHAPTER 12

Campaigns

C ampaigns are an investment with potential risk and rewards. In this chapter, I will cover startup campaigns as a pure business process with a focus on the steps that trigger decisions. If you've read the marketing budget chapter, then you are familiar with asset allocation. Campaigns are similar to a marketing budget in that you allocate assets and spend money. Whereas your marketing budget is judged quarter by quarter, your campaigns move at the speed of light.

A live campaign is an open faucet. The running water is cash that is being spent every minute. When a campaign is running, expect to track it 24 hours a day, 7 days a week. Campaigns don't magically stop when you leave the office (unless you manually stop them or automatically set them to run at certain hours).

I love the excitement of a live campaign. Even at night when my mind is on other things, it is hard to resist the temptation of opening a campaign tab and checking out the results. Campaigns are a numbers game. Make the right decisions and you will deliver quality leads. Make the wrong decisions and you will waste your budget.

3 Ways to Pay For a Campaign

There are three main ways to pay for campaigns – CPC (cost per click), CPL (cost per lead) and CPM (cost per impression).

CPC – You pay for every click. It could take 10 ad impressions or 100,000 ad impressions. This is the most commonly used campaign payment model because it is results based. CPC only tracks the first click to an external page. At that stage, the "clicker" sees your content and is faced with another option to click again.

CPL – When the person who clicked on your ad the first time is taken to your landing page and decides to fill out your form or whatever your call to action is, they become a lead. CPL costs a lot more than CPC as it takes a lot more ad impressions and initial ad clicks to generate one lead.

CPM – You pay per impression served. It doesn't matter how many times people click or how many leads you generate. CPM is great for branding and for B2C.

When I ran my advertising-based website, I used the CPM model. Why? "I don't want to base my income on your marketing skills," I would tell advertisers. "Pay a fair price for use of my real estate." Tracking ads was a lot easier – I only needed to track ads that I served and not what "happened to them" afterwards. My business costs were low, so I could afford to charge a competitive price.

In those days, we didn't have modern tracking tools. Every banner server would provide different numbers on the same results. CPM was more efficient. In today's data-driven world, everything can be tracked at the micro level. CPC quickly took over as the standard advertising payment model.

As you know, the main platforms for running campaigns are LinkedIn, Facebook and Google AdWords. There are hundreds of ad and affiliate networks. The word counts and specifications of advertising content change over time, but the essence is the same.

Short text and an image with a link to a page that you determine. It may be text/image/text, text/image or even image/text or just text.

Let's run through a few scenarios of LinkedIn. In the first scenario we are promoting a blog post. The campaign leads to a blog post that has a form right under the blog content. In the second scenario we are promoting an eBook. The campaign leads to a form to be filled out in return for an eBook. In the third scenario, we are promoting "Get a Demo", a form that leads to a live demo or an email or phone call from sales to schedule and run a demo.

Campaign Decision #1

Start at the end and begin with the landing page. Consider the 3 stages of the funnel:

Stage 1 – Tips and how-to content

Stage 2 – The challenges and pains

Stage 3 – How to choose a new vendor, why a certain product feature is vital, x vs y comparisons

Stage 3 leads are inherently more "ripe" to speak with sales due to the content they have expressed interest in. You are what you click! Stage 2 leads are interested in your industry and require nurturing. Stage 1 leads are at the opening of your funnel and are beginning their journey into your funnel.

For scenario 1, write a new blog post or choose an existing one. The stage of the funnel determines the type of content. A blog post landing page can cover any of the 3 stages of the funnel. When prospects read your stage 3 content and aren't ready yet, they can read other blog posts and website content and hopefully become a lead later on.

Consider the call to action button below the blog post. Campaign prospects are clicking and reading the blog post. Now what? An eBook? Get a demo form? Contact us? Think in terms of cash – how much will you be paying LinkedIn or another platform for the click? For LinkedIn, expect to pay $5-$8 per click. If it takes 20 people who click to fill out a form, that's at least $100 per lead.

For scenario 2, choose the eBook based on your business goals. Likewise, consider the 3 stages. You may want to A/B test the eBooks used in campaigns in order to learn which work best. An eBook landing page should be minimalist – don't distract from the goal. Decide which form fields you absolutely need and which you can live without. At one startup, we only asked for name, email address and company. By skipping phone number and other fields, our eBooks were distributed to many people who weren't ready to give us their phone numbers. The eBooks gently pushed them along the funnel with professional content.

Make sure your eBook has a killer title! You are paying a lot of money for people to read your eBooks. The one you choose had better have a catchy title with content that delivers a powerful message. Stretch the envelope as much as you can without going too far. I once promoted an eBook titled, "Lessons From The World's 3 Worst Ever ERP Disasters". The world of ERP is as far as one can get from a James Bond movie with an explosive ending. But ERP systems are expensive and notoriously challenging to upgrade. The title and content added color to what is considered a boring topic. Take away the boredom – ERP runs the world's largest companies. Without ERP, your favorite drinks and snacks won't leave the factory or distribution point.

Another idea is the "Master the art of ..." eBook title. Others title ideas are "The Ultimate Guide To ...", "How To Stop ... From Driving You Nuts", "3 Killer ... Features That You Can't Afford To Miss", "The ...

Buyer's Guide", "5 Signs You Need A New ... Vendor", "How To Choose A ..." and "The x Features Checklist". Try fitting some of these titles into your world and see what you can come up with.

For the third scenario, we are sending those who click on the campaign straight to a get a demo form. That is a huge step. Eventually there is no avoiding this step. In startup marketing, you need to be able to push even a small percentage of your leads from funnel start to finish on the spot. This is a very tough skill to master. It is one thing to get someone to download a PDF and quite another to ask for what they know will be a sales call. If you have a "Free Trial" instead of or in addition to get a demo, you are still taking leads to the end of the funnel to give information and try something. Not easy!

By the time you start running campaigns, you have created a lot of content that makes the case of your startup. Take out your best ammunition for the get a demo landing page. (Again, exchange get a demo with whatever your specific end of the funnel call to action may be.) Spend hours designing every pixel and word of the landing page. Consider what form elements you need. Every added field lowers conversions. Without enough fields, you won't capture quality leads.

At a few startups, I merged the "first name" and "last name" fields and had my technical team make necessary form and CRM changes. You can ask for a corporate email address. If you are creative, the corporate email address also signifies the company.

Another idea is to mix scenario 1 and 3. Send leads to a blog post that has a get a demo form underneath. If they're ready to convert, great. If not, they can continue to read more content.

Campaign Decision #2

Next comes the ad content. Take a good look at the landing page that you're using for the campaign. This is your source for ad content. Summarize it with a powerful headline in the allotted words. If images are allowed, carefully choose an existing image or a new stock photo. An original image is best, but your best illustrations may not appear clear as a small sized campaign image. If you go the stock photo route, be bold! There are over 100 stock photos that your leads have seen many times. Images need to have a "wow" affect and be closely aligned with the text.

One lesson I learned working with a great marketing professional at a successful startup: Make sure the ad and landing page are nearly identical. The content of the ad is the headline of the landing page. Use the same image in both. Why? When someone clicks on your ad, they don't know what they are about to see. Similarities between ad content and landing page add a sense of "comfort" to visitors.

Think of looking at an ad on the glass window of a store that mentions a sale. Entering the store, you expect to see items on sale. If not, you will leave.

Create a few versions of your ad copy. Your next campaign decision will take us to running and testing your ad.

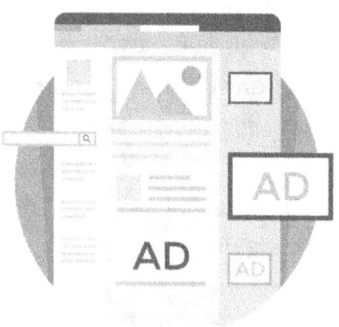

Campaign Decision #3

LinkedIn, Facebook and other advertising platforms offer amazing ways to target leads. Before you run a campaign, consider all of the options. On LinkedIn, there are many filters – job title, industry, experience, company and more.

One trick that has worked well with a few startups that I've worked with is to target by company. If you are targeting companies that have less than 1,000 employees, work with sales to create a "wish list" of 50-200 companies that you most want to sell your product to. When you create the campaign on LinkedIn, type in or paste each company name. This is what I call "super targetting". At a company of 100 people, the few who login to LinkedIn every day will see your ads. With this method, I was able to bring in a constant drip of top quality leads to sales.

Whatever the platform, consider how you can "super target" and almost pick and choose your leads. Explore the advertising platform. They are intimidating to look at the first time. Get acquainted by "clicking around" and take note of all options. Read up on the latest best practices for advertising on your chosen platform. The details change but the overall process remains the same.

Another similar trick works on Facebook. Facebook lets you upload spreadsheets and target them one-by-one. When your sales team returns from a conference, you have hundreds of new leads who expressed interest in your startup. Upload the spreadsheet to Facebook. Facebook will identify 20-30% of them. The more fields you have on your spreadsheet, the more people Facebook will find.

Now you are super targetting people who are a lot more interested in your offering than a random sampling of Facebook.

A third trick for super targetting is to create multiple audience groups. Let's say you are targetting two different decision makers – one technical and one business. Create two audience groups for your campaign on LinkedIn or whatever advertising platform you are using. Don't mix them until you know how they each perform.

The same goes for any two distinct factors in your target audience. One group for one industry, one for another. One group for directors and one for vice presidents.

Speaking of groups, LinkedIn has Groups covering every possible business topic. When preparing a conference campaign, you can target members of a specific conference group. Even when you are not promoting a conference activity, you may want to promote your eBook or solution to members of a conference group.

There are many roads that lead to sales qualified leads. Consider each one of them and test your good ideas. Become an expert at grouping and targetting audiences within the confines of advertising platforms.

Campaign Decision #4

It's money time! You have a budget, landing page and ad copy and are ready to run a campaign. Before you do anything, make sure your funnel works from a technical standpoint. Fill out a form from different pages and make sure everything appears properly in the CRM.

Whether you have a huge or small budget, start off small. Run two different ads that lead to the same landing page. The minimum daily budget on most platforms is usually around $10 a day. Start at the minimum. Run both versions of your ad copy under the total minimum. If clicks cost $5-$8 each, you will get a few clicks per day. It will take a week to start to see a trickle of numbers.

Campaign Decision #5

Now that the campaign is running for a week, it is time to start analyzing the results. How many impressions did each ad receive? How many people clicked on the ad? How many clicked on the ad and filled out the form? Did any go further and speak with sales or actually run through your demo or free trial? Check Google Analytics to see how long visitors spent on your landing page.

Hopefully after a few weeks, you will know which ad copy works best. Why did it work better? What funnel stages do your ads reflect?

The second part of campaign decision #5 is to make changes to your ad copy and landing page based on what you are able to learn from the campaign. Look for the "cork" that is preventing more leads from moving through your funnel.

Imagine you are a detective in a "Whodunnit" mystery. The "crime scene" offers a few possible hints – the ad itself, the landing page, the form, the alignment between ad and landing page and even design. There is a whole science on the best colors to use on landing pages. Read up on the latest best practices and come up with your own ad performance tricks. At this stage, the budget is low, so you can afford to experiment.

Campaign Decision #6

Campaign decision #6 is to scale up the most successful version of the campaign. Take the budget from $10 a day and raise it to $20-$50 a day. If you have the luxury of time, add $10 a day per week as you continue to track and analyze results.

You are spending thousands of dollars a month at this point. Keep a close eye on every dashboard – Google Analytics, CRM and the platform where you are advertising. Look for good and bad deviations at every stage – impression, click and lead.

Continue to improve results and keep adding to the budget until you reach your limit.

Seek More Campaign Sources

Go beyond LinkedIn, Facebook and Google AdWords. Look into smaller news sites and platforms. If your startup covers a narrow niche, the best sources of advertising may be indie news and websites. Be creative – you can run banners, text ads and thought leadership articles.

The more sources of quality leads you have, the better. Don't rely on one or two major advertising platforms if you can help it.

Final Note on Campaigns

Run this process through in your head and with your marketing team members. Map it on out paper before you spend money. Once campaigns arc running, you are expected to react quickly and it won't always be during work hours.

Stay in touch with sales throughout the campaign and ask them for feedback on each lead. This has often helped me to fine-tune my campaigns.

It sounds like a lot of work – and it is. On the good side, once I've done all of the above steps and have an excellent performing campaign, it is a pleasure to let it ride the wave.

CHAPTER 13

Conferences

Startups invest a lot of money and resources into conferences. Marketing professionals are expected to produce the conference – from the most minute details to how to generate a high number of quality leads for sales teams. A conference is a major production.

Conference Logistics

Once your startup decides to attend a conference and you know you are hosting a booth, get in touch with the organizers. They will have a web portal that you will login to. A good conference portal will have an online checklist with all of the things you have to do and when. Print this out and/or create your own checklist. List it in order of when you need to do things – conferences are full of deadlines to meet.

If you have the luxury of beginning your conference preparations 5-6 months ahead of time, you're in good shape. Take a look at your list of things to do and start taking care of what you can do now. Arrange regular meetings with your startup's "conference team". Make sure everyone is communicating regularly on logistics.

At this point, make decisions on your own logistics. What size and type of booth do you need? What kind of demo will your sales team be offering on a large screen and in person? Some conference booths include a small meeting suite. Consider the furniture your booth needs and anything else beyond the booth itself. What TV's, tablets and laptops will you need?

If you require communication between devices, be ready to deal with slow or no internet on the conference floor. You may want to create a special demo that doesn't require internet in order to work.

You can often purchase tables and chairs from the conference organizers, but it may be very expensive. At every startup I've worked at, we would arrange for someone to head out to a local store and spend a few hundred dollars. If you need a large TV screen, it may be cheaper to buy a new one than to rent one for the day. You can always do a raffle and give the TV away.

If you are running an event at your booth – say, cocktail hour – know what you're getting into. Nothing is cheap at a conference and there are often high minimums for every item or service.

When it comes time to ship things, you can ship to the conference, to a hotel or to someone who lives nearby. If you ship to a hotel, call ahead of time and let them know.

Before the conference team leaves, make sure they have everything they need.

The Booth

Building a conference booth can be fun – especially if you have a partner at your startup to work with. You will also need your designer, who will be tasked with transferring your brand from your website to a booth.

Whatever the size of your booth, you need to convey and communicate a "killer message" in big letters so everyone can see it. What one short phrase says it all? What kind of design do you want based on your experience and your brand's look and feel?

After choosing and designing a booth, consider what items the booth requires – tables, chairs, brochures, demo rooms and demo screens.

Get input from your sales team – they need to be comfortable working at the conference booth.

Ordering and creating a booth takes time. Prepare the design as early as possible so you're not shipping your booth at the last minute.

Printed Assets

You definitely want to prepare brochures, datasheets, case studies and whatever other high quality content that you have. Decide early and start producing the content – the words and design. Find a printer, agree on the details and have everything printed and ready to go weeks before the conference. Better to print too many than too few.

Marketing & Sales Strategy

Months before the conference, meet with your CEO and sales team and discuss your marketing and sales strategy. How will you attract people to the booth? What will be your message? While you don't want people reading from cards, you do want your sales team saying roughly the same thing.

The bottom line – who are the decision makers that you want to attract to your booth? Who are the influencers? What are their job titles? Determine what industries and types of companies you want at your booth. Know who your sales team will be hunting ahead of time.

Go out of the box when it comes to bringing people to your booth. Your startup is spending tens of thousands of dollars. Spend a bit on marketing your booth. The conference organizers will offer ways to market your startup to conference visitors via email, their app, printed directories and whatever else they can come up with. Consider the options.

There are conference vendors who offer marketing services. There are many creative ways to attract an audience – a game, prizes, large screens, a demo of your product and many others. Speak with your colleagues at other startups, especially those who have used local conference vendors and maybe you will discover a new way to bring quality people to your booth.

Every major conference offers the ability to scan name tags. Usually this is an added cost. Yes, scanning everyone at your booth is a good thing to do. You can end up with a list of 1,000 people and if you don't know who is a hot lead and who was just passing through, you missed the point. The goal is quality over quantity. Better to have 50 hot leads than 1,000 random people.

The Conference Decision Maker Game

Among the thousands of people on the conference floor, your sales team is looking to speak with a few hundred. They will spend all day shaking hands and meeting people in order to isolate the all-powerful DM – Decision Maker. It takes a lot of small talk to get to the right person or people. What can you do to speed up the process?

One way to isolate Decision Makers and get people quickly in and out of your booth is "The DM Game", or simply "The Game". Offer a prize at your booth – something big like a toy helicopter or a teddy bear (parents love to come home from conferences with gifts for their children).

Booth visitors stand on line and when it is their turn, they approach a tablet on a stand – like on a TV game show – and fill in their details. Before the conference, you and your team create a backend – a form with a seemingly random prize generator. You can set it to give 1% of your booth visitors a prize. More importantly, you can set certain fields in the form to automatically win – by company name, title, industry or anything else that is on the form.

You pre-define who you want your sales team to speak with. When that person comes to your booth to play your game, they will win and a sales person takes them aside to give them their prize and to speak with them – hopefully to offer them a live demo of your product.

There are many iterations of "The Game". If you have the in-house capability, you can create it yourself or have a conference vendor produce and run the game for you. Many conference vendors have their version of "The Game" ready to go. You just need to supply a few tablets and do a few test runs – in your office before the conference and at your booth.

Communication

Create a WhatsApp group or other closed group for the conference team – including those of you who are attending and those who are not. Everyone needs to be in sync with live information. If you are working with conference vendors who are in on the action, add them to your group and make it clear to them what situations will require their immediate attention.

As a marketing professional, you will often stay home while the sales team flies to the conference. You are the backstage producer. If you have any say in it, make sure that the team flying to the conference has a good hotel and budget for good restaurants. They work from morning to night before and during the conference and often have to deal with jetlag and long flights. They deserve to be treated well.

Surprise!

If you plan everything head of time and with skill, everything and everyone should arrive on time. The booth will be delivered and setup and everyone will know exactly what to do. Be prepared for surprises. Something may not arrive or you may need an additional tool or device. Make sure the conference team has a Plan B for quickly resolving these issues. A delayed flight can also slow things down. Hopefully, everyone is scheduled to arrive early enough so a few hour delay won't make a difference.

Be especially prepared for surprises when it comes to your demo, TV screens, internet connection and anything you are presenting at the conference. Make sure everything will work under tough conditions (a slow connection).

The Most Important Part of a Conference

After the conference, everyone eventually arrives home – tired and hopefully with hundreds of high quality leads. Organize a post-conference meeting. Listen to everyone's experiences and stories. You will always come up with things you can do better and more efficiently next time. Your sales team will probably have its own post-conference meetings where they delve into the details of the leads.

Prepare ahead of time and determine who collects lead lists from sales people, and when that person creates a master lead list. Within days of the conference, you should have a master lead list.

Your lead list will include the obvious information. Make sure it has who at your startup is responsible for the lead. Rate the leads as hot, medium and cold. Have your sales team update an online version of the lead list so everyone can work with the same document and the CEO and VP Sales can track progress.

Once every sales person has their list ready to go, the most important part of a conference begins – reaching out to the hot leads and closing deals. Of course sales will reach out to all leads, but it is these hot leads that sales professionals are most confident they can sell to "now" or in the next quarter. Both sales and marketing have an interest to sell to the low hanging fruits and pick up quick wins.

The normal sales cycles for post-conference efforts is 3-6 months. If you have a large lead list, hopefully your sales team will have a constant flow of conference leads going from medium to hot to purchase order. Marketing professionals should speak with their colleagues in sales to see what content they need in order to facilitate closing deals. Often a relevant case study will help a lead get others on his side to sign off on a deal.

Your startup's VP Sales will be running the show when it comes to closing deals after a conference. Get involved in the conversation where you can. There is a sense of handoff here from marketing to sales. If you did your part, the sales team will have an easier time closing deals.

CHAPTER 14

How to Track and Analyze Results

T racking and analyzing the results of marketing activities is a complex aspect of startup marketing. There are endless dashboards, graphs, percentages and comparisons to make. With a budget comes responsibility. Marketing owes the CEO and CFO full accounting for spending and results. The marketing budget determines what is spent where and tracking and analysis determines the ROI of the money spent.

Everything is Measurable

Every marketing activity is measurable. The first layer is the website, which you have full control over. The second layer is campaigns and outside platforms which also allow you to track and analyze results. In the early years of the internet, tracking campaigns was challenging. Everyone used different definitions and tracking tools. Today, the major marketing platforms have become "standard candles" accepted by the industry. They include Google Analytics, Google AdWords, LinkedIn and Facebook.

In this section, I will cover how to build the initial foundation of tracking and analysis. It is vital to start off simple and accurate. Some of this is discussed in other sections; here my goal is to help readers to lay the foundation for accurate tracking and analysis from day one.

Google Analytics & the UTM

Before Google Analytics, website owners had to pay hundreds of dollars per month for website tracking. Every platform offered varying results. Google Analytics shook things up – it is free and is the industry standard of website analytics. Yes, there are more powerful tools out there that you can pay for but a small startup (and I believe every business) should begin with Google Analytics.

On the technical side, a piece of code is placed inside the header of your website. Web developers can do this quickly. From that moment on, Google Analytics tracks website traffic. Most marketing professionals are very familiar with Google Analytics. For those working in other startup fields, here is what Google Analytics can tell you:

- How many people visit your website in any given time frame
- How many people visit each page
- How much time people spend on each page
- The bounce rate for a specific page. The bounce rate is the percentage of all sessions on your site in which users viewed only a single page.
- Geography, languages, operating systems, mobile users, types of devices
- Entry and exit pages – the most common pages where people entered your website and the most common pages where people left your website
- The most common paths through your website – it is incredible to see a depiction of the most common user journeys through a website. When you have accumulated a year of traffic, this page can really help you to analyze the flow of your funnel.
- Track who filled out a form or any interactive content

Meet the UTM

Let's say you are running two campaigns that lead to the same link. How can you track which one is performing better? Meet the UTM, Urchin Tracking Module. Look for UTM's in links on your URL bar – it is the part beginning with the "?" with letters and numbers immediately after the website address.

For example:

https://www.example.com?utm_content=blog&utm_medium= social&utm_source=linkedin&campaign=campaign1

You determine the fields – content, medium, source and campaign. An additional field is a term for isolating search terms. You can skip a field if it makes things easier. When working at a small startup, choose one field and give it a campaign name – facebook1, linkedin2. When things get more complex, you can expand your UTM fields. For a company with dozens of live campaigns and inbound links, one or two UTM fields will let you track everything. Experiment with UTM's and come up with your own best practices.

On the technical side, find a UTM spreadsheet on Google and copy it to your side. Save a blank copy for future use. Every time you distribute or post an inbound link to your website, create a unique UTM. Paste the link onto your UTM spreadsheet, fill in the fields based on your needs and copy the UTM-included URL.

The Goal Completion

Google Analytics has a very powerful feature called the "goal completion". Every time someone fills out a form on your website, they are taken to a "Thank You" page which acknowledges their action and communicates what to expect next. By setting up goal completions, you can track every form filled out on your website and view the numbers on Google Analytics.

Your CRM contains the results of every form filled out. Goal completions allow you to compare forms filled out (leads) to website visitors. Better yet, if you use UTM's, you will know where the lead originated from (if the lead began their journey via a campaign or link).

Let's say you have a classic Get A Demo form on your startup's website. Create a new goal completion on Google Analytics. Give it a name and enter in the URL of the thank you page. (Create a unique thank you page for every different type of form.) Fill out the form yourself and see if you appear as a goal completion.

Goal completions are leads. Tracking and analyzing leads are critical for improving performance and ROI.

Keep on Top of Google Analytics

Bookmark Google Analytics and check it every morning. When you run a campaign, check every few hours or even keep the tab open. Google Analytics will even show you when people are on your website in real-time and where they are from. This can be exciting to watch when you are running a major campaign or activity.

Look for goal completions. Compare them to CRM leads. If the numbers don't match, have your web developers or CRM professional look into it.

CRM Tracking and Analysis

The CRM is where leads go. I can't emphasize enough how important it is to start off simple. You want leads to flow from forms to the CRM, and for everyone in your company (especially sales) to be able to track and review leads.

Every new Google Analytics goal completion is a new CRM lead. Determine who gets notified when new leads are generated. Take a look at the CRM's built-in dashboards. Most offer a few different "views" of your lead data. Choose the one that fits your needs, taking your CEO and VP Sales into account.

Bookmark a page on the CRM that you want to see first. When you are analyzing results, open the CRM tab to the right of the Google Analytics tab.

Campaign Tracking

When you run a paid campaign, the advertising platform provides you with dashboards and dozens of ways to view and analyze results. I've found that LinkedIn's advertising platform user interface is easiest for beginners. A non-marketing professional can easily understand campaign results on LinkedIn. Google AdWords and Facebook are more complex – expect to invest an hour on each to get acquainted with the basics and a few hours to be somewhat comfortable.

No matter where you run your campaign, a screen will show you the following details:

- Ad impressions
- Ad clicks
- Clickthrough rate (impressions/clicks)
- Social interactions – You usually don't pay for a "like" or "share" and these are freebies thrown in. How this works depends on the advertising platform. Social interactions on your campaigns help them to be seen by a bigger audience.

- Cost per click (assuming the cost per click model). Some advertising platforms will also display the cost per impression and cost per lead so you know how much these two are valued at based on your cost per click. Likewise, if you are paying cost per impression, it is good to know how much each click costs you.
- Total money spent

Bookmark the advertising platform's page and this is the third tab, to the right of the CRM and Google Analytics.

More Tracking and Tabs

For every major marketing tool you use, you have a new tab open on your browser. This includes Marketo, Hubspot as well as other advertising platforms. When you are spending money for a real-time activity, track and tab it!

Create a Master Spreadsheet

All of the tools and opened tabs are "the trees". Create a forest – a spreadsheet – and track results in one place. Identify the key indicators and fields in each tool. Add all necessary fields to your spreadsheet. Focus on the big picture for your first version:

Total website visitors
Total leads
Leads from campaigns (leads with a UTM)
Organic leads (leads without a UTM)
Total sales qualified leads
Total sales from paid campaigns
Total sales originating from organic leads
Top converting pages (the pages that trigger the most forms filled
    out)

Add fields for each campaign. For example –

LinkedIn total spent
LinkedIn clicks
LinkedIn leads
LinkedIn sales qualified leads
LinkedIn sales

You can add as much information as you want. Start simple and scale up. Update it weekly or monthly, depending on your pace. This spreadsheet is a source for the marketing quarterly report.

It is critical to view top level results on one page, within one view.

Over time, your marketing activities will expand and there will be much more to track. Be your own editor and decide how to track the bottom line of each new activity within your master spreadsheet. Show it to other colleagues and get feedback – especially from your CEO and VP Sales.

CHAPTER 15

Marketing Best Practices Per Sector

There are many startup sectors and many ways to categorize them. In this section, I cover the most common sectors. Whether you work in a specific startup sector or not, it is important to understand the subtle and not so subtle differences within the startup ecosystem. Marketing professionals are expected to be capable of moving from one area to another. Ask yourself what would you focus on during your first month and first quarter at each startup? Note the differences in the content requirements and the types of campaigns that tend to work better in each sector.

Ad Tech

Ad tech is a mature market compared to blockchain and influencer startups. Advertising is a huge business and continues to grow. Unlike startups which offer potential revenues, ad tech companies make real money. The margins in ad tech are perhaps slimmer than in other B2B industries, but ad tech startups make up for this with large volume.

The tracking and analysis technologies available today can be so powerful they are frightening. If you are not a marketing professional in the know, Google "most powerful ad tracking tools" and expect to be shocked at what advertisers are capable of doing in order to convert leads.

In most cases, your decision makers are marketing professionals. They are the ones who decide to buy advertising tools. The funnel is short and sweet – you aren't selling something that costs $100,000. Pricing for ad tech tools is typically per use or monthly + per use. You want leads to quickly start a free trial or view a demo and get started.

Automotive

Automotive is a fast growing sector. Automotive companies realize that the car of the future will be based on powerful technologies. Today, your car is able to warn you when another car gets too close. In the future, your car will drive you to work. There are even cyber security startups that specialize in securing cars. Other startups improve electric car charging, monitor the health of drivers and passengers (fatigue, sleepiness and stress level), trucking and even voice activated services.

Automotive startups work in a closed ecosystem. Decision makers are automotive professionals and other automotive startups. When targeting a large company such as Mazda or General Motors, dive in deep and learn who the most relevant people and titles are. General Motors has over 180,000 employees and you can't afford to target everyone. If you are marketing an automotive technology, a large car company probably has an innovation team. Reach out to them – online and directly.

When an automotive startup is looking for a few large companies to embrace their technology, the funnel goes from marketing to sales and stays at sales (or business development) for a long time. It takes months of hard work in order to obtain the equivalent of a purchase order. Automotive startups build complex software and hardware. Marketing is the easy part! Closing a deal and getting the other side to onboard with your platform or solution is a major effort.

Big Data

Big data startups sell sophisticated products and services to mid and large sized companies. The magic that a good big data startup can provide is worth hundreds of thousands to millions of dollars to the other side. The products can be complicated to explain to someone not familiar with modern big data.

For big data, focus on creating deep, detailed content. Decision makers are data junkies and they do a lot of reading before they pick up the phone or fill out a form. Most people at a company are not in charge of obtaining new big data tools. Expect to target a variety of seniority levels and job titles.

An automotive company may not expect an automotive startup to have a 500-page website, but a big data decision maker does expect this from a big data startup. Be prepared to write a lot of quality content.

Blockchain

Blockchain startups are the new kid on the block. It is interesting to see where blockchain and bitcoin will go. One side says it is the future; the other says it is yet another asset bubble. Bitcoin aside, blockchain technology does have many potential real world applications. The best part of watching the blockchain sector is that it is unpredictable. No one knows where blockchain will be in 5 years.

Blockchain startups move at the speed of light! They usually have offices in co-working spaces and the founders will be younger than in other startups.

Decision makers can be both consumers and business. A blockchain startup with a coin offering will be targetting consumers, many of whom behave as investors or businesses in that they are not buying into your offering for fun – it is an investment. Blockchain technology startups will be targetting other blockchain or fintech startups and maybe other traditional financial service providers and institutions.

As opposed to big data startups, the funnel is quick. Your website displays who you are and what you do. You collect information and offer a way to "get started" with whatever it is you do. You don't need a huge amount of content in order to check every necessary box and feed your prospects with information.

A blockchain platform or tool can have both consumers and business professionals as their targets. Start off with the lowest hanging fruits and conquer converting leads in one area at a time. Blockchain startups are often loaded with cash (as long as it lasts!). Don't be tempted to skip the low budget testing phase when advertising. It's not just about money, it is about craftsmanship.

Cloud

Like ad tech startups, cloud tech startups have been around for a very long time. Unlike ad tech solutions, cloud startups typically sell high cost solutions and services. Mid and large sized companies rely on the cloud for running both internal and external processes. Cloud startups allow companies to scale and leverage their cloud presence – and thereby increase productivity, sales and ROI.

The decision makers and influencers for cloud startups are IT and R&D. Consider what you offer and who is likely in charge for procuring cloud solutions. Decision makers may also be on the innovation or even product teams, depending on your offering.

The length of your funnel is determined by the scope and price of your cloud offering. Create eBooks and case studies to make your case. The cloud is an easy story to tell. Make a direct connection between your products and your leads' expected return on investment.

Consumer

Consumer startups is a broad category, covering every startup that sells to consumers and not businesses. This includes hardware, software, online tools and parts of other sectors such as travel tech and fashion tech.

Consumers don't expect 500 pages of content like in the big data startup example. Consumers are looking for concise content that talks about one thing and one thing only – value. Value for money or value for lifestyle improvement – you choose. Remember the feature, benefit and dream concept? With consumer startups, focus on the benefit and dream.

Your decision makers are segmented. Certain demographics are more likely to buy your products and services. Identify and target them in your first campaigns. "Build audiences" of different demographics and perfect the art of converting them.

Create a lot of fun, engaging content for consumers! Most consumers love to read something informative that makes them smile. The type of products and services you offer determine how much fun you can have. Generate viral content and spend a lot of resources on social media. Not everyone is active on social media, but those who are moderately and extensively active can make a huge difference in your marketing efforts.

Create a message that is unforgettable for consumers.

Development and Agile Tools

Scrum, anyone? Development and agile tools are obviously geared towards R&D and Product. For non-R&D people, it is amazing to learn how deep the world of modern development is. There is a mantra (agile). a method (scrum) and a way forward (sprints). There's a lot more going on over there in R&D beyond someone coding. IT, R&D and QA collaborate in an "agile orchestra" that requires tools and processes.

Decision makers are R&D, IT and QA team members and leaders. Of the three, who is more likely to need your product? Who is the influencer? With development and agile tools, the funnel is likewise quick – often leading to a free trial.

The funnel may be quick, but the content had better be deep. Development and agile tools decision makers are flooded with new tools and platforms every week. Create a clear flow from feature to benefit to dream.

Ecommerce

In early years of the internet, the hardest part of ecommerce was building a good shopping cart and making sure everything worked. Today, ecommerce is a busy ecosystem full of influencer, automation and shopping tools which increase traffic and revenues. Ecommerce isn't going anywhere. If anything, it is overshadowing the real-life retail experience.

How many times have you visited a store to look at a product, only to end up buying it online?

The decision makers and influencers for ecommerce startups are obviously ecommerce businesses. Your targets are the marketing department. When marketing targets marketing, watch out! The content is usually flashy and colorful. The bottom line in your messaging is about making more money.

Education

Whether the education bubble is real or not, institutions of learning spend a lot of money on technology. In the US, the inexpensive SaaS Chromebook laptops have gained traction. Distance learning is no longer a new trend. Beyond degree programs, many people take online courses for a certificate or just to learn something.

Both online and offline educational institutions require tools. Years ago, I worked at a load testing software tool technology company that was over 10 years old at the time. The biggest customers were university IT departments who require detailed load testing in order to have a successful registration week. They spent tens of thousands of dollars to test their university registration systems. A crash or slow down during registration week could be a punishing event. There are so many other types of services and tools that help universities. There are education startups that focus on alumni associations, fundraising, resource management, human resources and of course all things financial.

Decision makers for education startups are university employees and their vendors. Often, the target is the IT department. If your startup does something for human resources, it could be IT and human resources. Expect decision makers to be both non-technical professionals and IT. This means your content has to have both a business and technical angle to it. Figure out how to target both with the same words and phrases.

It is not easy to get a purchase order from a university. Sales teams work hard with the university side, often speaking to many levels of people in the chain of command. Conferences are a big deal in the university ecosystem. There is a culture of university professionals attending one or more conferences a year. Expect to prepare marketing materials for conferences. For some education startups, conferences may well be your main source of leads, or a major one.

Fashion Tech

Fashion tech is an up and coming startup sector. Many of the tools and services connect with ecommerce and many connect with social media. Some of the coolest startups enable online fashion retailers to connect with the most relevant influencers, acting as a matchmaker between the two. Other fashion tech startups let you turn on your camera and see how a new pair of jeans or a shirt would look on you.

One major challenge that a few fashion tech startups are trying to resolve – every fashion label has its own standard for sizes. When it comes to jeans, I know my size and buy one size up in length. But there are subtle differences in waist sizes between brands – especially when it comes to slim and other sometimes unique styles. Shirts are easier – you know if you are small, medium, large or extra-large. Shoes? A size 11 Air Jordan isn't necessarily equivalent to a size 11 Adidas.

Fashion tech startup targets are typically online fashion retailers as well as brick & mortar retailers looking to improve their online presence. Targets are very specific in this case. Create a list of your top 100 or so targets and start running campaigns on LinkedIn and other platforms.

The fashion tech funnel leads straight to a free trial or demo. Content is very important to fashion tech. Retailers splurge on social media and creating viral content.

Fintech

Fintech is a promising sector. Many fintech startups connect ecommerce websites to credit providers and lenders. Instead of a slow process, the credit check, approval and checkout can be nearly instantaneous.

Online banking is nothing new. Securing online banking and adding new features which allow bank customers to do more with their money are both major areas of fintech. Other fintech startups include digital payment platforms, insurance (price comparisons and services), microloans and peer to peer lending.

Fintech startups target financial institutions (including credit, lenders and processors). Decision makers are most likely from the business. Financial decision makers are all about benefits, as opposed to the features. Financial startups often have a complex offering. Create a simple story that will be the basis for your messaging and content.

Healthcare and Wellness

Most of us want to improve our health and wellness. There are startups that create apps and even devices which help consumers and patients with a specific ailment or issue. The medical device ecosystem is a major industry on its own. Consumer apps and services are also a mature business by now. Health and wellness startups also help hospitals and clinics with hardware or software backed by a powerful technology.

Healthcare and wellness is a promising technology sector that should continue to grow at a fast pace. Leveraging technology to save and improve lives is a wonderful thing. Society (people, governments and organizations) spends a lot of money on healthcare. I don't know if blockchain will be around 30 years from now, but I do know that healthcare startups will be.

The funnel for health and wellness startups is long when marketing to the business. No one buys anything medical for their business without a thorough process. The content should reflect this. Take a deep breath and determine who your decision makers and influencers are. It will vary from startup to startup. Assume you will be targetting large organizations and be required to drill down with your campaigns.

Testimonials and case studies are the best way to connect with prospects. From day one, generate and distribute as many as you can every quarter.

Information Security

Information security startups have been around since the beginning of the internet. People and organizations have to protect critical and non-critical data. For banks that offer online banking, security is paramount. Ecommerce sites require a secure method of payment – and customers who have enough faith to type in credit card information.

Most information security startups focus on the B2B side of things, offering tools and services for security critical data.

Decision makers for information security startups are IT, application directors, QA, R&D and of course CISO's and information security departments. The content is tricky. Your story is, "Prepare for a disaster. What happens when a hacker breaks into your system and does ..."

"Are you ready for ... to happen?" You don't want to scare people with your content, but there's no going around the "avoid disasters" theme even if you give it a lighter touch to it.

The information security funnel is full of touch points – whitepapers, eBooks, demos, videos and webinars. How do you stand out in a crowded field while maintaining a conservative brand?

Internet of Things

Internet of Things, or IoT, is a fascinating field. I love reading about it. Imagine your refrigerator sending you a message that your ice cream expires on Monday, giving you the perfect excuse to binge eat your Ben & Jerry's. If it is winter and you live in a cold city, imagine using your phone to turn the radiator or air conditioning on. Turn on your water heater when you leave work so you have a hot shower when you get home.

Other internet of things startups enable heavy machinery and even warehouse shelves and items to communicate.

The smart home is a major trend and opportunity for internet of things startups. Many people have already connected their light fixtures and are able to turn lights on and off via smartphone. Smart plugs let you add connectivity to nearly anything that you can plug in to a wall. Other IoT startups focus on home security.

Internet of Things startups have two possible audiences – business and consumer. The business target is often a reseller, consultant or distributor. Not every IoT device is meant to be installed by the end user. For basic smart home devices, the consumers can handle the onboarding.

For the B2B side, targets constitute a very small niche. Create a spreadsheet with your 100 best companies to target. For B2C, focus on the IoT enthusiasts and hobbyists. They are the early adopters who convince their friends to join the IoT revolution. Early adopters love features and the dream. Their friends, the regular consumers, prefer a mix of benefits and the dream.

Privacy and security are legitimate concerns with regards to IoT. The more potentially invasive the product, the more focus on allaying those concerns. I'm not worried that my refrigerator will record me, but I don't want a live speaker in my home. A lot of people don't mind and the first generation of family room IoT products are gaining traction.

IT

IT is a mature ecosystem as disruptive IT tools are needed as soon as the first computer is unboxed at a business. Startups cover everything from collaboration to help desk to automating IT tasks and software. I worked at an IT startup and learned that the competition is fierce. IT professionals are flooded with offers to try new solutions every day.

Decision makers and influencers for IT startups are obvious – the IT team. For help desk solutions, the customer success team may also be decision makers. Consider who benefits from your offering. Thought leadership articles posted on respected news sites may be more efficient than LinkedIn campaigns. Ghost write articles in the name of your CEO, VP Product or CTO. There are many IT review sites – get your products and services listed and accumulate positive reviews. The funnel leads straight to a free trial.

Marketing, Financial & Business Solutions

Marketing startups are responsible for the amazing marketing tools that we use. Think of Marketo, Hubspot, OKToPost, MailChimp – marketing automation, email, funnel, content, landing pages and marketing performance tools. Financial and business startups include the CRM, human resources, resource management solutions. There are even SaaS tools which help sales professionals with leads.

Decision makers and influencers are easy to discern here based on your offering. HR tools are used by HR professionals. Marketing tools are used by marketing professionals. Dig deeper into the specific title and seniority of the people most likely to benefit from your solution. Create a lot of content that focuses on the immediate benefits. "What is in it for me from day one?"

Do whatever it takes to convince decision makers to begin a free trial. Some free trial offers don't require a credit card, others offer real use and not just a demonstration of features and user experience.

Mobile

Mobile startups generally fall into three broad categories – apps, analytics and IoT. There are BYOD (bring your own device) startups that help corporations and government organizations deal with employees using personal devices at work. BYOD solutions include allowing work apps to be used on personal devices, but the data is stored in the cloud or on-premise servers. At one BYOD startup that I worked at, I came up with the slogan, "Zero Data On Device".

Everyone is familiar with mobile apps. There are apps for every topic under the sun - lifestyle, business, games, health, business, inventory, hobby, entertainment and more. Some apps are free and offer paid services – the freemium model. Others have a one-time fee and others go with the monthly or yearly subscription model. Many of us have an ongoing subscription to a music streaming service.

Apps collect a lot of data. Apps analytics startups offer tracking and insights with regards to app usage and increasing conversions and ROI. All of the major apps use a tool or many tools in order to glean insight and act on it.

IoT fits in the mobile category as well for one important reason. Mobile is a major touch point for Internet of Things. No one wants to give you a new controller to walk around with. You are already carrying the universal controller – your smartphone. When a startup plans on connecting any "thing" to the internet, they create a mobile app on the other side.

Mobile startups target both business professionals and consumers. Video games have a different marketing approach than mobile analytics.

Generating leads from apps and converting free users into paying users is a detailed science. Work with a professional who knows this domain.

The freemium funnel is straight forward – users download your app and begin using it. The small percentage of super active users who pay for extra services and goodies are funding your business. Of course a freemium app needs a lot of users. The challenge is in getting someone to pay for it. When I check out an app today, I don't believe anything I see in the reviews – that business was corrupted years ago. I watch a YouTube video of the app in action.

Mobile analytics startups have a more defined target audience – marketing departments at companies with successful apps.

Mobile has one advantage over other startup categories – once a user in inside your app – even on a free basis – you have their full and undivided attention. Apps don't have browser tabs.

Social Media and Influencers

It is incredible to see how the world of social media influencers has grown to the in-depth industry of late. Every business has influencers. Consumer facing businesses especially rely on influencers to generate hype, viral content and grow their audience. Ecommerce sites are more than happy to outsource these activities and automate them. Like it or not, social media become an entrenched part of the consumer experience.

Influencer startups are an interesting niche. Influencers aren't naïve – they invest time in their craft. Everyone in is on the game – consumers know what is going on and enjoy the experience. Influencer startups connect the dots between business, influencer and consumer.

A powerful social media or influencer solution has a killer built-in message. What you do should "wow" your decision makers. Leverage the perfect mix of benefit and dream. For the funnel, do whatever it takes to get your most likely early adopters to use your solution and "create" your own influencers. Leverage their experience on social media. A social media or influencer startup should know how to "eat the food they cook" and quickly build up an audience of free trial and paying users.

Travel Tech

Travel tech startups do a lot of things – automating everything that goes on an airport, hotel booking and infrastructure, vacation rentals, property management, car rentals and every part of the travel experience. Some of these are B2B, B2C and many are a mix of both. Consumer travel tech startups solve many challenges of travel and allow travelers to transfer unused tickets and points to other travelers.

Travel tech targetting is based on the service provided and identifying the travel industry professionals and companies who need your offering. Everyone enjoys travel. Travel content isn't as hard to write as ERP content – generate a lot of content and promote it on social media and with paid campaigns. If you are in a specific niche within travel tech, create a list of your top 100 prospects and work with sales on a plan of action.

CHAPTER 16

Agile Startup Marketing

Much has been written about devops, scrum and agile. R&D, IT and QA are inter-connected and work is done in sprints. Before agile R&D, one side would work for months on one aspect of a project. They would pass it off to the next team (say, QA or IT) who would make or require technical changes and improvements that would set things back to square one, or close to it. This was called "waterfall". Progress was slow.

With the agile sprint, large projects are split into shorter pieces. When one side stops the process and adds something to the mix, the other sides don't have to begin from scratch. In simple terms, agile is a measuring process that calls for four steps:

- Do it
- Analyze it
- Make changes
- Back to the beginning

With R&D devops, there are specific steps related to releases, testing and feedback, but the big idea is that coders, IT and QA to work efficiently in tandem.

Marketing Devops

In startup marketing, we have our big 3 – content, campaigns and sales. Content is how we present our startup to the world; it is the food that we want a specific audience to eat. Campaigns are what we do with the content in order to generate interest in our startup. Sales is the prime goal of marketing – turning interest into purchase order.

Let's compare marketing to R&D devops:

- Content = R&D
- Campaigns = IT
- Sales = QA

Content is our code. Campaigns are implementation of the code. Sales are performance.

Agile Marketing

When you start working at a startup, there are a lot of things to do. Messaging, a website, PR, campaigns, conferences and of course quarterly reports. Look at every major project with the eyes of a CEO who has a tight deadline.

A website is a major project, but can you finish it in 30 or 60 days? Learn how to say, "Let's do this after we launch" and create a wish list for additional website features and pages. Determine what you need on the website in order to start generating quality leads. Produce a good, functioning startup website and set quarterly goals for adding new content and design elements.

When you begin to run free social media campaigns, create a simple process that lets you post your content and move on. Build up your first few hundred followers and "super fans" organically one week at a time. When you are ready, you can add layers of social media tools.

Paid marketing campaigns require an agile mind frame. The path is to start with small campaigns, find the sweet spot and scale up.

Innovate, implement and analyze!

As for conferences, the earlier you begin planning, the more you afford yourself to take care of logistics in short sprints months ahead of time. Choose, design and build your booth as early as possible.

Content should also follow an agile cycle. Determine what your biggest content needs are, produce a batch of content and leverage it in campaigns and other marketing activities.

Keep all of the marketing wheels spinning together at a fast pace.

Be your own editor and learn how to shorten processes. Be honest and admit that you can't afford to be a perfectionist. You can spend six months creating the perfect startup website, but no one will give you six months to get the site up and running. By the time you hit six months, you need to be way past the website and initial campaigns and at the scaling up stage.

Quickly determine what you do hands-on, what others on your team will do and what you will outsource to vendors. A CRM consultant may be able to get your CRM up and running in a few days. That depends on how complex your initial funnel and needs are. If you are starting with Salesforce, don't expect to complete implementation in a week. If you really need to start off with Salesforce, you have wonderful problems – starting off with millions of dollars in revenues. Otherwise, go with a CRM that fits your needs and most of your wishes.

Speak with your designer before embarking on a major project and make sure that they have the free time. Set time estimates for every "design sprint". WordPress developers work quickly – adding website features can be measured in minutes, hours or days.

Once campaigns are fine-tuned, you may find yourself in an interesting situation – you are generating a constant stream of sales qualified leads, your budget is steady and your CEO and sales are pleased. Let your campaigns run on auto-pilot – keep an eye on them – and move onto other things. When campaigns are performing well with little effort on your part, produce a few case studies or try out a new marketing tool.

When it comes to adding marketing tools, add them one at a time. Implement and learn how to use every new tool. See that you are getting value and the tool works with your funnel and that it delivers results. Learn which promised features end up adding value and which don't. Prioritize your goals. Does sales need a jolt of fresh leads? Is social media the key to increased relevant traffic?

I love reading about and testing new marketing tools. Sometimes they work and sometimes they don't. One tool that I tested let us see the IP addresses of many of our website visitors. In most cases, we could discern what corporation was visiting our website, but obviously not the job title or person. I realized that even if I knew who the person was, it wouldn't do me any good. On a first visit, they aren't ready. Live chat tools, on the other hand, have exceeded expectations. They aren't expensive and some sales people love using them to speak with returning website visitors. The right marketing tools can make a big difference. But not big enough to justify holding up every other marketing activity.

You may find that working at home one or two days a week adds to your productivity. Some people need an office and others are capable of working on the couch or sitting at a desk at home. When you work at home, set high productivity goals and try to match and beat them. With few distractions, you can have a "marathon day" or days where you complete many "marketing sprints" in a short time thanks to no commute, no meetings and no long lunch breaks.

Constantly analyze your progress before others do it for you every quarter. What processes are taking longer than expected? What is moving along faster than expected? How fast are the marketing team's sprints as compared to vendors? What is the source of slowdowns?

A good startup executive knows how to quickly identify processes that take too long, what to cut and how to get the maximum results.

That's agile marketing.

CHAPTER 17

8 Signs Your Startup is in Trouble!

If predicting which startups would succeed were easy, we would all be millionaires. Many successful startups have experienced every last one of these trouble signs yet still made it to the finish line with a successful exit. Many more don't.

Poor Communication

Good communication is especially important with a small group of people who are spending someone else's money. Everyone owes it to investors to be both productive and polite at the same time.

Most startups have weekly meetings. Everyone should speak for 3-5 minutes offering a summary of activities. Unless there is a major project, no topic should be discussed for more than 15 minutes. Know when a department specific topic should be "taken offline" and dealt with later.

Long meetings that end up in shouting matches are a bad sign. Let others do the screaming. Company meetings are a way to gauge your CEO, who is ultimately responsible for shaping your startup's culture.

Processes Never End

The never ending process. It goes on within corporations all the time. Startups can't afford never ending processes. From the minute that the first seed money is deposited into a bank account, the clock is ticking. Everyone owes it to investors to be agile.

Be on the lookout for unnecessary projects as well as critical projects that are never completed. Remember the basic startup cycle:

R&D -> Product -> Marketing -> Sales -> Money.

R&D develops a technology. Product turns the technology into a product. Marketing markets the products. Sales sells the product.

Every department needs to hand-off their completed part to the next department on time. Group projects should be well defined. Sometimes projects take longer than expected.

When every project takes longer than expected, you have a problem.

Mediocre R&D Team

R&D should be held up to the highest standards. Without the R&D team, there is no startup. A mediocre R&D team leads to a mediocre or failed startup. For startups without a product team, R&D is fully responsible for turning the technology into a finished product.

If after three years, R&D hasn't built a solid product, it is a sign your startup is in trouble.

Overspending

Enjoy the steak lunches and Nespresso machines while they last! Every CEO knows how to spend other people's money. The best CEO's know how to balance spending other people's money while delivering a high return on investment.

You can't always control overspending in other departments. Ordering a hamburger when everyone else is ordering prime rib won't stave off future budget cuts. Be aware of the spending culture at your startup.

Overspending at a startup – especially after a period of a few years without a solid product - is a very bad sign.

Awkward Product

On paper, the technology looks great. When you test it yourself, it is cool. But something in your head tells you that the product is awkward. Hopefully it is just you. There are two other options – the product needs fine-tuning, or the project is so awkward that it will never be used.

I've seen startups fall in love with their prototype like children at a candy store. They brush aside legitimate critiques and tough questions are never asked at product meetings (when they even occur). Everyone just knows they are sitting on the holy grail.

If you can, show your startup product to a friend or colleague at another startup. Do they confirm your fears?

Some startups begin with a product that doesn't quite do it and take a few years to get it right. These startups have two players who turn the vision into reality – CEO and VP Product.

When your product is awkward and no one is doing anything to improve it, you are looking at a bad sign of things to come.

Customers are Never Onboarded

Marketing delivers leads to sales. Sales identifies the best leads and the first purchase orders arrive. What's next? Most startups don't have a customer success team or even manager at this early stage. Who does sales hand off the baton to?

Sales can't onboard a startup's first customers (or 100th). When the first purchase order arrives, the CEO should work with the COO, VP Product and VP R&D and form an onboarding team. The attitude should be "all hands on deck" – there is nothing more important to the startup than successfully onboarding the first customers.

I was shocked beyond belief when I once saw a CEO and COO display a laid back attitude towards onboarding their first potential customers.

As the onboarding process involved complex hardware systems, I knew they needed to fly out to the newly signed customers and spend a week or more learning the ropes of product implementation.

They thought they could implement the first customers remotely and I knew it was a bad sign.

Of course phone calls are enough for implementing most SaaS solutions. The more complex the hardware, the more the possible need for managing initial implementations in person. R&D and Product can learn a lot from being there. A good startup CEO knows how to bring the initial customer onboarding process to a successful end.

Too Many Years in the Desert

Some startups spend years at the seed level. This buys time when dealing with a new and complicated technology. R&D may require a few years to flesh things out and extract something that a product team can sculpt into a product.

There is a risk in staying too long at the seed level, or "friends and family" stage. Friends and family investors don't have the same standards as a venture capital firm or investment group putting down a Series A investment. It is a lot easier for the CEO to answer to a few angels as opposed to venture capital. The Series A contract itself is full of goals, partnerships and results monitoring that seed level startups never experience.

Furthermore, there is a tendency for seed stage startups to "walk the desert" without a finished product. When venture capital comes in, they set a deadline for the product and are more interested in the marketing and sales rollout.

Startups that run from angel to angel without a firm backer face long odds of success.

A Narrow Niche

Some startups solve problems that we don't even consider to be problems. Many internet platforms excel at enabling us to skip steps and publish content quickly. Some tools are redundant or only needed by a narrow group of professionals.

As an investor, I have set of rules that I use when deciding whether or not to invest in a company. One of them is, "Is the product line an ecosystem?" Disney is a huge ecosystem. They own content, the pipes that the content is broadcast on and a lot of places that people visit. A camera or translating tool isn't an ecosystem.

Ask yourself – how wide is my startup's dream? When a real person uses your product, which of the following is their reaction?

- Not useful
- Could be nice
- Will help sometimes
- Often helpful but only in specific circumstances
- Very useful
- Useful to the masses

Where is your startup? Is your startup forming an ecosystem or adding an essential part to a major ecosystem?

A narrow niche startup can become the next unicorn (a privately held startup valued at over $1 billion). It can also be a bad sign.

CHAPTER **18**

A Passion For Technology

Marketing professionals come in all shapes and sizes. There are automobile marketing professionals who work at car manufacturers and their PR agencies to brand and market new cars. There are health care marketing professionals who hawk healthcare services. Every niche requires someone who markets the products and services.

That "someone" is expected to know about what he or she is marketing. Automotive marketing professionals probably know more about cars than I do. They are likely interested in cars as a hobby and have even test driven a few exotic cars. Cars have been around for a long time, and someone who wakes up and "accidently" finds himself marketing cars can read up on decades of knowledge and experience about cars – models, parts, features, benefits and how to market each.

There is no such luxury in high tech.

Even The Beatles Didn't Have Smartphones

High tech in its current form exists since the 1990's. Ford and GM's experiences marketing cars in the 1960's and 1970's may be relevant today to modern automobile marketing professionals, even if advertising takes place on different media. A startup marketing professional can't look back to the 1960's to see what they did two generations ago. Two generations ago, even The Beatles didn't have smartphones.

Technology was done by large government organizations, universities and Dow Jones components (think IBM).

Marketing books and CEO autobiographies can inspire you and even offer a relevant path to solving a modern challenge. But no details. As a startup marketing professional, you are on your own.

In many cases, startups are not only creating new products, but new industries and sectors. The more the founders are pushing the boundaries, the more marketing professionals are expected to work and succeed in unexplored territory.

Not only is your startup disruptive, the marketing tools you are using are often startups as well!

High Tech is as Deep as it is Wide

There are ecommerce startups, marketing automation startups, automotive startups, mobile app startups, B2B SaaS startups and much more. Under each of these are potentially dozens of sub-categories with hundreds of startups filling each one.

You may find yourself working at a startup in a field that you didn't know existed. You won't have a wealth of information to read.

You can't market something that you barely understand.

The Solution – A Deep Understanding of Technology

Startup marketing professionals must have a deep understanding of technology. There is no shortcut.

A deep understanding of technology will help you in many aspects of your profession. If you want your VP Product to take you seriously, you had better know your tech. Startup product professionals expect you to understand not only your startup's underlying technology, but technology in general. A well-rounded and strong tech background that includes "things you've done" and not just "things you've read" is vital in order to build strong professional relations with Product and R&D.

On the practical level, it will help you to translate your startup's features into benefits.

Explore!

Technology websites are your playground. Spend hours a day reading about and test driving technologies. Here are some basic technologies that you can "learn by doing" at home.

Client/Server

Install a basic web server on your laptop. Configure it and "host" a website so you see the front and back end of the web. The same for FTP. Create a local FTP server and experiment with it. Client/server technology – even old stuff like FTP and IRC – is the building block for many new technologies.

WordPress

Create your own WordPress site. You don't need your own domain for this – just host it for free. Choose a theme, add a few plugins. Check out the settings. Try to find the most interesting plugins and install them. Maybe you'll find a few that can help you at your startup and you didn't even know they existed.

HTML

Learn the basics of HTML. Become familiar with basic HTML and PHP code. You don't need to be a coder, but you should be able to look at an HTML page, recognize what you see and make small text edits and formatting changes.

"Back in the day," I had to know HTML. There were no CMS's when I founded my first startup in the 1990's. Eventually WordPress came along and it was a pleasure to work with such a powerful tool. Knowing HTML and how WordPress works has helped me on countless occasions. When I can't solve it myself, I can at least isolate where the issue is.

Knowing HTML and WordPress raises the level of the conversations you have with web developers and other members of your team.

Gadgets Galore

Explore everything you can about gadgets. Lucky for you, there are so many types of gadgets out there waiting to be explored. Gadgets are very relevant to startup professionals because you will be exposed to both hardware and software and what happens when they "share the same space".

Laptops and Chromebooks

Start with laptops. Learn all there is to know about the specs and latest trends in laptops. You probably know about Ultrabooks, but did you know why non-gamers are interested in gaming computers? Gaming laptops are chock full of powerful hardware and often have insane designs.

Even if your startup gives you a laptop, buy your own. Read about the latest "killer laptop features" and find a few that you want on your personal laptop. Years ago, I bought a Windows laptop with a touch screen. It even folded back so I could use it as a tablet. The experience was awkward – it was too heavy to carry as a tablet, but it was cool to be able to touch the screen while typing. Today, laptops with touch screens are much thinner than the bulky ones from 2014.

Chromebooks are a fascinating laptop category. Chromebooks do one thing – they run the Chrome browser. I bought a Chromebook when they first came out and had a great time using it for a few years. Chromebooks are cheap – mine cost me $199 and most go for under $500. They are light – there is no fancy hardware. Basic hardware and a browser. Are Chromebooks more secure than Windows laptops? Why have Chromebooks become popular in education and not in business?

A Window Into Windows

I've met technology marketing professionals who barely knew Windows. They weren't familiar with Control Panel or Settings. They had never done a defrag, DOS or command line?! They couldn't troubleshoot a printer problem.

Don't go this route. Learn Windows!

Windows has improved vastly over the years. Remember the "blue screens" when previous versions of Windows would crash? No operating system is perfect, but Windows is the tool you will likely use on your laptop for the rest of your career.

Dive into Windows – see what's in Control Panel and Settings. Look for the obscure, but useful features. Become familiar with installing a printer and other hardware. Personalize your Windows laptop with themes, colors and sounds.

Windows has a firewall. Learn how it works and how to add and remove exceptions.

Go Beyond Office

You probably know Office and that's a good thing. Learn how to edit audio and video files. You just need to know the basics – download a free open source software, and create and edit a few small projects. Find a short piece from a song that you like and create a ringtone for your smartphone. Learn how to convert audio files to different formats, such as FLAC and MP3. What is compression in audio and video and how does it help and how does it affect quality?

Go Mobile

Mobile covers a huge chunk of technology and will keep growing. You already own a smartphone. Buy a tablet and experiment with it. Connect it to other devices. I once bought an 8 inch Windows tablet for under $80. It included a one year Office subscription, so the tablet paid for itself. It was amazing to see Windows running on such a small screen.

Android tablets are great – there are excellent models that run for under $200. Better yet, tablets last a long time – they stay at home and they don't age as quickly as smartphones because you just need it for the browser and to run basic apps.

Look for interesting apps and see how a tablet is practical for you at home.

Go beyond the tablet and consider other common mobile devices – ear pieces, wireless earbuds, noise cancelling headphones and earbuds, and of course storage devices.

Backup Your Life

There are many ways to back up your data – in the cloud, external hard drives, USB drives, SD and micro SD cards and more. Read about them and come up with a plan. Look into the SaaS backup services and see how they may or may not be able to help you. What new backup technologies are hitting the market?

Linux

For a period of a few years, I had a second computer which ran Linux. It did various things for me – ripping CD's faster than my Windows desktop computer and running resource heavy software that runs smoother on Linux than Windows. Most non-technical professionals have never used Linux at home. There is so much to learn from trying a second operating system. Linux is a technology unto itself.

Get a low end laptop and install the latest popular flavor of Linux. Configure a web server and other types of internet services. Try a bit of everything – graphics, Office and Office alternatives, browsing the web – and compare it to your experience with Windows.

Experience command line. You can do this in DOS too. Command line in Linux is hard core! A lot of what goes on in technology has roots in Linux – you can't measure how much actually using Linux will help you with concepts and applications later on.

Technology at Home

Technology begins at home! Consider what new technologies are available for the home. Do you want a device that listens to you and assists you? What new music hardware technologies are available? Learn about IoT – Internet Of Things – and how it can help you at home with electricity, appliances and security.

Devices in the home are interesting because they touch a raw nerve – privacy. The balance of technology and privacy is a challenge for many startups. As consumers, we want all of the benefits of technology, but we are increasingly uncomfortable with how our data is obtained and shared.

Marketing Tools

There are many categories of marketing tools. Marketing professionals should experiment with a few tools in every category. Create a free account and "try it out" where possible. The more you "do" and the less you watch on YouTube, the better.

I remember the early email marketing tools of the mid-1990's. The early SEO programs were fun to play with. Today, we live in a SaaS world and we don't download marketing software as often as in the past – if at all.

Marketing automation has matured – it is scary how tracking leads is done. Another chapter in this book discusses marketing tools. Here, I encourage the reader to experiment with marketing tools from your personal laptop. If you create a WordPress website, connect a few marketing tools to your website.

Know Your Technology

Your goal should be to obtain a deep understanding of a wide variety of technologies. Do this by "doing" and not just by "reading and watching".

Apply any useful technologies that you come across in life. Never stop experimenting with new technology on your own. The startup world moves at the speed of light and you are expected to keep up with it.

You can't imagine what technologies you will be working with and marketing in ten years. You can watch the future one step at a time with a curious, hands-on approach.

CHAPTER 19

Risk and Reward

Startup perks and benefits are legendary. One startup in particular comes to mind. The kitchen had two huge industrial sized refrigerators. Every morning, a delivery van showed up with boxes of fresh food. Eating breakfast or lunch was like eating at a good deli. We also had "food cards" worth $220 a month that were accepted at every restaurant in the area. Every Thursday, we were treated to a wonderful happy hour – Domino's Pizza, chocolate fondue, an ice cream bar.

The company had a culture of a good work-life balance. We worked hard and also had periods where we could go home a bit early. The company was filled with the cream of the crop in every department and on top of that, it was a very pleasant place to spend the day.

One day, we awoke to news of an exit. The news spread and everyone gathered for a company meeting. People had high expectations for their stock shares. Someone asked the CEO, "How much is our stock worth?"

For most of us, it wasn't a lot. I was only there a year and had no illusions or expectations. The founder deservedly received a lot of money. The product team members, who had been at the company for years and were responsible for creating a very useful ERP solution were well compensated (with terms that had them agreeing to stay on for a number of years in order to prevent brain drain). The longer you were at the company, the more you were compensated. Those who were at the company for 2-3 years and weren't executives were disappointed with the value of their vested stock shares.

"It is all about risk and reward," replied the CEO. "Years ago, startup professionals worked in old office buildings and brought sandwiches to work. Startups didn't have much money to pay them so no one made a lot of money until the exit and in most cases there was no exit. You are all paid well and work in a wonderful environment. With less risk comes less reward."

The CEO was 100% right.

Those of us who work in startups and technology companies are very well compensated. Not every startup has a lounge with pinball games and a country club sized kitchen. Not every startup tests your will power when it comes to hot, dripping chocolate. Startups function in a very competitive environment. The perks help them to recruit and retain the best talent.

A few years earlier, I was at an IT startup. The perks were wonderful – espresso machines, food cards that let me eat at restaurants every day, taxis to and from work for those working on weekends, and a generous amount of vacation time.

The startup was growing steadily but not at an astronomical rate. There were no illusions that we were headed toward an exit. If and when this startup has an exit, perhaps only a handful of people will own a significant amount of vested shares. Meanwhile, hundreds upon hundreds of young IT, marketing and sales professionals were well compensated and learned valuable professional skills during their time at the startup.

At another startup, we worked in a two-story home in a quiet upper class neighborhood. I had a view overlooking the yard. The R&D team showed up once or twice a week. We ate lunch at expensive steak restaurants. After lunch, most people went home. Eventually we moved offices to a downtown area known for being a startup and technology hub. The offices were empty a few days a week as we worked at home much of the time.

I had a lot of flexibility on my marketing budget and teamed up with the sales director to quickly figure out how to generate sales qualified leads. We could both see that people weren't communicating and important processes – like onboarding the first customers – were never completed. Eventually, the startup ran out of seed money and never received a Series A investment.

We were well compensated during our time at the startup, we had a perfect work-life balance. And we had no exit. Re-roll the dice and do it again!

When you consider the future of your career, you want a good mix of salary, perks, opportunities, professional growth and a good work-life balance. Exit compensation comes in last. Unless of course, you are willing to give up on compensation and join a startup as a co-founder or investor. In that case, your risk and potential reward are higher.

Aspire to participate in many successful exits during your career. Maybe one will be big, maybe a few will be good enough to make a difference. Every exit experience is a badge of honor. Expect to take risks in joining startups that don't pan out. When it's over, take a short break and do it all over again. Don't focus too much on the exit. Be aware of your compensation level, your stock shares and how they become vested. Keep your eye on what you and your team need to do each quarter.

Good luck and many successful exits!

About the Author

K enny Sahr grew up in Miami, Florida, where he founded his first internet business. In 1996, Kenny founded the popular SchoolSucks.com website. Kenny was featured in Time Magazine, NY Times and 60 Minutes. He has served as VP Marketing at a number of startups. Today, Kenny resides in Israel where he is a startup marketing executive.